STILTE

STILTE

THE DUTCH ART
of QUIETUDE

MIRJAM VAN DER VEGT

New York • Nashville

Worthy
Hachette Book Group
1290 Avenue of the Americas, New York, NY 10104
worthypublishing.com
twitter.com/worthypub

First Edition: October 2021

Worthy is a division of Hachette Book Group, Inc. The Worthy name and logo are trademarks of Hachette Book Group, Inc.

The publisher is not responsible for websites (or their content) that are not owned by the publisher.

The Hachette Speakers Bureau provides a wide range of authors for speaking events. To find out more, go to www.hachettespeakersbureau.com or call (866) 376-6591.

Print book interior design by Bart Dawson.

Library of Congress Cataloging-in-Publication Data
Names: Vegt, Mirjam Van der, author.
Title: Stilte : the Dutch art of quietude / Mirjam Van der Vegt.
Other titles: Stilte. English
Description: Nashville : Worthy, 2021. | Translated from Dutch. | Summary: "We all long for moments when we can slow down and for opportunities to be still. Life can get hectic, as we continuously hop from one thing to another. Days are often filled with too much noise, anxiety, and confusion. What do you do when the life you created isn't what you expected it to be? What can you do to slow it all down? Author Mirjam van der Vegt encourages each of us to focus on stillness and literal silence, creating space for moments of peace in our crazed everyday lives. Originally published in Dutch, Stilte reveals tips and tricks to bring mindfulness and calmness into your personal daily practice. Rooted deep in the Dutch culture, this book will teach you how to experience the benefits of silence. Just as the Dutch do!"-- Provided by publisher.
Identifiers: LCCN 2021023287 | ISBN 9781546015789 (hardcover) | ISBN 9781546015772 (ebook)
Subjects: LCSH: Contemplation. | Quietude.
Classification: LCC BV5091.C7 V4413 2021 | DDC 248.3/4--dc23
LC record available at https://lccn.loc.gov/2021023287

ISBNs: 978-1-5460-1578-9 (hardcover), 978-1-5460-1577-2 (ebook)

Printed in the United States of America

LSC-C

Printing 1, 2021

CONTENTS

PREFACE

QUIET NOW...

Shush; you have opened a book on silence. It's a shame, really, to write words on these pristine pages, for by doing so, I break the silence. Still, the letters are slowly filling this page, as I want to share with you the value of quiet in everyday life. I was deeply moved by silence, or, more particularly, by the One who speaks to us in silence, more than you could ever imagine. You know, I am a real busy bee, ambitious and moving here, there, and everywhere. Then, suddenly, I was brought to a stop in the middle of my hectic life, only to discover: There is more—so much more. Encountering this quietude, I discovered the full life! You will read more about this treasure hidden in silence in the Introduction that follows.

Ever since the discovery of that treasure, I set out in search of ways to make "slowing down" a part of my life. Following the publication of my first novel, *Shadow Flight*, I started organizing meetings called Evenings of Silence. Together with a musical friend, I toured the Netherlands as we hosted evenings filled with quiet, calming piano music and exercises in silence. How silence affected people! We were often asked, "But how am I going to put this into practice at home, this 'cultivating of silence'?" Forty varied Keys on how to "let life *be*" are presented in this book.

Silence is crucial to understanding life itself. I am weary of words. Let life just breathe, keep your mouth shut for once, let life be. The Dutch word "tegen-woordig" [present] is literally translated as "against words." It has taken on a different meaning for me: Sometimes life goes "against all words," it needs no words, it surpasses all words. That is when I remain silent.[1]

—Daniel van Santvoort, abbot of the
Cistercians of Caldey Island

Before you read on, here's a little test. If you answer yes to more than one of the following questions, this book is definitely for you.

- Are you a true multitasker? Is this you: While talking on the phone I do other things at the same time. I watch the news and combine it with, say, making sandwiches.
- Do you often compare yourself to others?
- Are you quick to judge others or yourself?
- Do you feel judged by others and are you often troubled by feelings of guilt?
- Do you dislike airy silences and does the word "meditation" get on your nerves? Is your motto "levelheadedness and working hard"?
- Do you long for silence and quietness, and do others misunderstand this desire?
- Do you often think: How much longer do I need to carry on like this?
- Have your prayers to God turned into short prayers between daily activities, like they are literally squeezed in?

- Do you often tell yourself, "I should go on a retreat…if only I had the time"?
- Would one hour of quietude and room in your busy, hectic life make you happy?
- Are you more aware of the time you *don't* have than of the time you *do* have?

CONFRONTATION

I wonder if you will read on. It takes courage to do so. Initially, silence is gratifying, but our relationship with silence can come to seem like a confrontation. So much so that people flee from it. Silence may seem boring, but it is very dynamic indeed. Silence may enable people to make big and small decisions that they didn't get around to before. An ambitious young man decided to devote his entire life to God, and he entered a monastery after having spent forty days as a retreatant at that monastery. A woman who had been abused experienced God's presence during a retreat. She was able to acknowledge her pain because she felt heard by God. After that, she was able to forgive the offender. An elderly woman dared to tell her mother no for the first time ever, setting her own boundaries. And, personally, after a period of experiencing stagnation, I dared to quit my steady job in the midst of an economic crisis. One week after that, my husband lost his job, so we faced an insecure future. But it all felt good—although everything surrounding us didn't seem right. Standing firm amidst chaos when grounded in silence—that is the fruit of silence. People prove able to make tough choices after descending the three steps of silence, which you will read more about in the Introduction. The descent of silence ends in your heart—a heart in which Jesus welcomes you to join with Him. To come home. To enjoy the love that He feels for you. A heart created by God, in which He longs to dwell, but that you easily rush past. Sound familiar? Maybe He is already waiting there for you to come around— waiting until you descend a few steps and say, "I am tired. I am looking for peace and quiet, and I can't do it on my own anymore."

THE GREATEST

Christians and nonbelievers alike are looking for inner peace. I once interviewed Dennis van der Geest, the Dutch world judo champion who won a bronze medal at the 2004 Summer Olympics. With great passion, he told me about his abundant life that he enjoyed to the full. When asked, "What would be the greatest thing that could ever happen to you?" he remained silent for quite a while. From that silence arose the following reply: "I would want to possess inner peace to enjoy my children growing up, without wanting to take part in a world of hurry and competition." Laughing, he added, "But I don't have time for that right now."

What Is the Greatest or the Best Thing That Could Happen to You?

Maybe Dennis's reply hits home. The greatest thing that could happen to you is real, steadfast inner peace. Something that enables you to resist the noise and the bustle in your life. Maybe you have been a Christian for years, but you are still struggling to find inner peace. You long for a peace that surpasses all comprehension and all circumstances.

"I don't have time for that right now," Dennis replied.

And how about you?

You may very well think: "It's a nice book to read or to give away as a present, but it's not for me. I really don't have time for that." But what if you compare its worth to a million-dollar prize? Would you take time to collect such a prize? Let's assume you would actually want to find time for the greatest thing that could happen to you. You are probably trying your very best to steer your life in the right direction and to build in extra time for rest. However, this turns out to be more complicated in practice. How do you free yourself from the yoke of time ticking away? When you seem to have a constant shortage of time, how do you create a pause in your own life? Rest and inner peace are connected. Quietude can be born in silence.

We often associate silence with an absence of words, music, or sound. This is certainly one aspect of silence. But you can be "still" and inwardly calm while a storm is raging around you, and when you are surrounded by a world filled with noise. This experience is about inner silence, an inner life undisturbed by outside noise.

JOURNEY

In her book *Time on Our Side*, Joke Hermsen, the Dutch philosopher, states the following on the concept of time: "Since the introduction of Greenwich Mean Time at the end of the nineteenth century, we have been living our lives by clock time. …Clock time has universal rules and a rigid subdivision in minutes and hours. By this, we are banishing the other, more personal or inner experience of time." In some cultures, the saying goes, "You have the watches. We have the time." This doesn't mean we need to throw away our watches, but there is quite some truth in the saying. We often seem to live under the "law of the clock," which in turn is determined by economic efficiency. Sometimes we seem to have forgotten we live under God's sun. The sun comes up and sets again and throughout the day it moves the daylight. Balancing clock time and inner time, as Hermsen puts it, is more of an art.

When you become quiet, it is not about clock time, but about the One you spend the time with. With yourself, with God. You are together in a beautiful entourage, in your own heart.

Anselm Grün, well-known monk and author, states:

You should stop running to get quiet....The German word "still" can be translated as "satisfying, soothing, feeding, nursing." A mother nurses her child, quieting down the baby screaming with hunger. In the same way, you need to quiet down your own soul, that is crying inwardly. When you stop running around, the hunger of your heart makes itself felt. Your heart needs to be nourished. You should give motherly attention to your heart to quiet it down. Many people are afraid of dealing with their unquiet hearts. They rather seek distraction, running from here and there. But their heart is crying out. It wants no distraction. It needs love. It wants to be cherished.[2]

Cherish your heart.
Want to join me on a journey?

—Mirjam van der Vegt

THE TREASURE IN SILENCE

Before we set out on a journey of silence, I will first explain something about the why of this journey. Why do we yearn for a handful with quietness, as the Bible puts it so beautifully in Ecclesiastes 4:6 (NKJV)? And why do some people, in their search for peace and quiet, go to such great lengths? The story of St. Seraphim of Sarov (1759–1833) is an extreme example of this. He is one of the most venerated saints in Russia and beyond. He lived as a monk for more than eight years, as a hermit for another twenty-five years, and in a locked monastery cell for yet another fifteen years. In the period he was a hermit, people started to notice the radiance of the peace he had found in silence. Thousands of pilgrims came to him and went home comforted by him and relieved from their doubts and worries. I don't think everyone is called to such a solitary life, but what a story! Certainly, there is a treasure hidden in this silence. Deep down in our hearts we all know this treasure is tangible. We are miners for gold, yearning for a nugget of pure beauty.

More Than You Can Swallow

The story of St. Seraphim is beautiful, yet it discourages me at the same time. Will it be so many years before I take hold of the gold? The way I see it, there are people who take less than twenty years and then there are those miners who seem to be born with gold in their hands. I found that God gives me room to learn, so I set off on my journey. But after an initial relief, it seemed like silence didn't gain me much; agitation, uncertainty, distress, loneliness, and restlessness were the symptoms that surfaced. Virtually everyone looking for the treasure will first have to deal with these emotions, as you will discover when you read more about the three steps of silence.

Gold miners took the rough of the journey with the smooth because they knew that finding the treasure would make them happy. Once they had taken a closer look at a gold nugget, there was no going back. This is altogether true for the treasure hidden in silence as well. In silence you will find what is paramount over all: love itself. All things on earth fade before love. As the Bible tells us in 1 Corinthians 13, even hope and faith cannot overcome love. Whoever has tasted this love has a good chance of drinking deeply from its well. 1 Corinthians 13 states the fruits of love; this is the treasure you find in silence. A treasure that enables you to remain peaceful whatever the circumstances. Who wouldn't want these fruits of love?

Patient | Kind | Does not envy |
Does not boast | Not arrogant |
Not rude | Does not act unbecomingly | Not irritable |
Not resentful |
Does not rejoice at wrongdoing | Rejoices with the truth |
Bears all things | Believes all things | Hopes all things |
Endures all things

Some consider love to be impersonal, a stream of energy floating throughout the universe. During my journey of discovery, I learned that this love is actually very personal: It is Jesus Who is God and Who is the inexhaustible source of love, together with the Holy Spirit. We are not searching for gold; we are searching for God. This shouldn't surprise you, as this is how God made us. The heart of every person contains a throne destined for Him, whether you like it or not.

Reflection

St. Seraphim of Sarov was considered a kind of god by some people. Luckily, we don't have to take on God's role, though we are called to be more like Jesus. In his book *The Inner Silence*, Fr. Jacques Philippe tells us to think of stillness like the surface of a lake. "If the surface is calm and tranquil, the lake will reflect the sun almost perfectly. The smoother the surface, the more perfect the reflection. If the surface is unquiet and turbulent, the sun will not be reflected in it. When the peace in our soul increases, God can be reflected in it, the better He imprints His image in us, the more His grace can work in us." Paul talks about this reflection as well in 2 Corinthians 3:18. When we truly see Who God is, we will be transformed into the same image, beholding His glory. In his devotional *My Utmost for His Highest*, Oswald Chambers states: "Let everything else—work, clothes, food, everything on earth—go by the board, saving that one thing. The rush of other things always tends to obscure this concentration on God....The severest discipline of a Christian's life is to learn how to keep 'beholding as in a glass the glory of the Lord.'" Let silence help you with this.

> In silence, you discover love.

HEADING OUT FOR REST: THE THREE STEPS OF SILENCE

Now that we have had a first crack at the gold, we want more! So let's start our journey of silence. It may be hard for you to get started, as your luggage is filled with burdens and thoughts. Why would you want to look for silence? It is easier to keep running than to pack your bags and take a time-out, heading for a journey with an unfamiliar destination. Supposedly, there is a treasure to be found. But then again, in the past so many gold miners returned home empty-handed. You may not be adventurous at all, and you may not feel like embarking on some new venture. Shaping your ordinary daily life may already be a challenge.

The good news is that this journey ends without luggage, and you can sit down whenever you feel like it. You're not supposed to climb Mount Everest; this journey is not a way up, but a way down, deeper into your heart. Taking a good guide is a sensible thing to do, and there is one available free of charge. It is a person who knows all about ways that go down and heavy burdens. Some call Him the quintessence, but He is more than that. How much more, you are to discover during the journey. As you have probably guessed, His name is Jesus. Mind you, He is not one to impose Himself on you. If you'd rather walk alone, He will honor that. He does make a promise, though: Whoever seeks Him will find Him!

The journey you are about to start on is a bit like the journey the first Christians took. Throughout the second century AD, some Christians fled into the desert because of persecution. There they discovered that silence, solitude, and moderation in food, drink, and sleep could provide receptive ground for prayer. Consequently, some of them moved even deeper into the desert and gained many followers. Eventually they founded communities from which Christian monasticism originated.

Like those second-century Christians, we, too, are traveling. Not because we are persecuted for our religious beliefs like the first Christians, but because the hustle and bustle of everyday life can be a threat to our inner lives. We are a bit like St. Benedict. He fled the city of Rome around 500 AD. Not because of religious persecution, but because he was tired of the "noise" of the city. He retired to live in a cave for three years, as he was longing for intimate contact with God. During these years, he learned that you need others to grow spiritually. Subsequently, he wrote *The Rule of St. Benedict*, starting the Benedictine monastic life that considers regularity, or discipline, and attention as its pillars. Benedictine life amid society gained popularity because it is proven to be effective as a way of life that facilitates contact with God. That's why you will find St. Benedict's instructions in this book.

On this journey of silence with its three steps, silence is not a destination in itself—as is the case in some forms of Eastern meditation. Silence is a journey within, deeper into your heart. A journey that takes you to an encounter with God.

Silence
is a song for two voices
wherein God and human touch each other.

—Guillaume van der Graft,
Dutch twentieth-century poet

During a short stay in a monastery, I came across a marvelous metaphor to describe this journey that stuck with me. I read it in a leaflet with inspirational quotes from various monastery residents. It amounted to the idea that silence consists of three phases or steps. The meaning of these steps became increasingly clear in the conversations I had with various monks in the months that followed. It's like literally descending the stairs and journeying from outward silence to silence within.

First Step: Relief

Many people are familiar with the first step of silence. After a busy period, there is a chance to calm down, finally…and you draw a breath of relief. Once out of the hectic pace of everyday life, you end up in a wonderful and quiet forest and you feel peace descending. Don't you love it, this quietude? People who often stay in a monastery recognize this. When you've just arrived and you unpack your bags in your plain room, all of it still feels pleasant enough. You are filled with eager anticipation. What will surface out of your heart after this first relief? Will God speak to you, or will He remain silent?

Enjoy the sense of relief on that first step. It is essential to include many of those brief moments of relief in your life. But it would be a pity if this forces you to ignore the deeper quietude. Right through the unquiet following the first step, there is another, deeper dimension to silence.

Second Step: Stumbling

Following the initial relief, silence can suddenly become terrifying. A monk once told me that after a few days of silence many people flee the monastery. The first step of silence was agreeable, but then the struggle sets in. In this context, Anselm Grün refers to the "spirituality of taking heaven by storm":

Nowadays many people have become fascinated too easily by spiritual paths. They think they can travel these paths without first having gone the difficult path of self-understanding, to discern their own drawbacks. The Desert Fathers warn against a spirituality that wants to take heaven by storm. We can easily share the fate of Icarus, who made waxen wings and plummeted down when he got too close to the sun. The wings we built before we have begun to face our own reality are really only made of wax. They have no lifting power.[3]

Anselm Grün tells us: If you want to know God, first learn to know yourself, including your dark side. That's what happens during the second step. And rest assured that God is with you throughout the entire journey as He promised He would be. We can take from this that in the light of God, you learn to know yourself. You need His Holy Spirit to bring out the dark side of your existence. The second step is about this dark side. All the things you had tucked away so neatly now suddenly emerge. You are preoccupied with grief, or mourning, or with everyday matters and feel deprived of your peace of mind. You become restless and make up distractions in order to avoid the silence.

The first time I visited a monastery with a group of people and spent the night there, it was quite hilarious to find out what was induced in us by this silence and quietude. Some of us could handle it really well, but others, to my surprise, became rowdy, grumpy, or miserable. Silence by seclusion may not at all be your way of drawing closer to God. That's possible. Still, I believe that at some point all people should be able to put up with themselves. Silence is an excellent method to test that.

> Just when I want my heart to go out to God, the dark side of my life is emerging within me. Then it is important not to push these forces aside but to focus on them. They surface for good reason.[4]
>
> —Daniel van Santvoort, abbot of the Cistercians of Caldey Island

On the second step of silence, judgment often predominates.

- *Judgment of the situation:* Why am I sitting here in quietness or just taking a quiet stroll? Shouldn't I be busy, making good use of my time? I'm sure I can spend my time in a much better way.
- *Judgment of other:* Why is he so successful and I am not? I work much harder than my colleague and she gets the credit. It's not fair.
- *Judgment of yourself:* Why do I keep on making the wrong decisions? I must be a failure because I still can't do better than this!
- *Judgment of God:* Why don't You take care of me? I don't hear from You. Take a look at all the misery in this world; why don't You intervene? If You care for me, then why is this happening to me?

Maybe you skip judging yourself and you're stuck with judging others. Whatever happens to you, it's always somebody else's fault. You decide that the sermon that touched you really only applies to someone else, for *she* is the one who still has so much learning to do. Do you realize that such a judgment often originates from a judgment of yourself? Why are you actually judging the other person? Are you trying to run them down so you look better? Is it easier to look at others than it is to take a look at yourself?

A Time for Everything

On the second step of silence, you can feel both judged and juror. There is only a thin line between these two. You call out, "Wretched man, wretched woman that I am!" Sometimes old pain from your childhood and your past will surface. You may become aware of your shortcomings and therefore you put on the "hair shirt" of the condemned. It's actually good to confess your shortcomings and to lay them out before God's throne, to admit: I cannot do this on my own. Forgive me for trying so often. Rather than walking around in this hair shirt of condemnation, you may learn that God has another garment in mind for you to wear.

> Your judgment of others often arises from judgment of yourself.

Something warmer and much lighter, which you will discover on the next step.

Some Christians claim you can just skip this second step of crisis. Jesus has died for our sins, and thanks to Him we can always wear a garment of victory. It is true that Jesus' work has been accomplished and finished. We no longer have to wear that hair shirt of condemnation. Our condemnation has been done away with because Jesus bore it on the cross. But while living in this broken world, we are handed that garment of condemnation—unnoticed and unsolicited. People say nasty things about us, or we are afflicted by illness, hunger, and abuse. Moreover, our ego often bothers us with pride, our passions distract us from love with jealousy, and so on.

Take some time to consider this and to have that garment removed from you. Bring your vulnerability into the open. Mourn for the pain you may have suffered from others. It's okay to mourn out of grief and brokenness. The Bible states:

> *For everything there is a season, and a time for every*
> *matter under heaven:*

A time to weep…
A time to mourn…
A time to tear, and a time to sew.

—Ecclesiastes 3

We don't live in the hereafter yet, where time is eternity. We are living on the earth, where the trees lose their leaves every year, where the rain fails to appear and the sun shines so fiercely the crops wither away in the fields. Living on the second step is like "grounding," understanding that you are dust, and to dust you shall return. And, just when you think you can't hold on for much longer, you suddenly hear a voice…

Third Step: Inward Silence, Living as a Beloved
"You are beloved."

Now it's as if the three-step staircase is turning. It is not a straight staircase; it's a winding staircase. On the first two steps you could still view your own earthly life, but now you are descending, and, as you hesitantly put your foot on the next step, a new scene unfolds. You see a path illuminated by a light. A glaring light that almost blinds you.

And then you hear that voice, tender yet powerful, telling you who you truly are in essence. "You are beloved. Come, the Teacher is calling for you." Now you can't help but walk on in awe, filled with marvel, falling to the ground. This is sacred ground.

It's like your heart is quenched with the purest spring water. It is swelling and expanding. You can barely contain it. Not only does your heart change, but your eyes have been metamorphosed as well, like a film of love has been cast over them. You'd think this makes your vision muddy, but your vision is even clearer; colors are brighter than ever before. Suddenly you understand you can rise and grab the hand of the One standing before you. Deep within you a song rises, one of peculiar sounds. Without articulating it, you know this is the person who will guide you to the source of all love. He will lead you to God. Your hand is enclosed by His, as if He encloses your whole being. He guides you to the source, but He Himself is the source as well. The beginning and the end and the road you must travel on. You would want to stay here forever.

Do you think this account is fuzzy or not realistic? That's possible. The peace God grants you surpasses reality. The above depiction is a summary of my personal experiences and of people I interviewed after they spent time in a monastery cell in their quest for silence. It is reminiscent of a conversion story, like it's your first encounter with Jesus. The message is one of descending from your head to your heart.

For a Christian, the ultimate object of silence is the source of love: God Himself. God who had so much love that He even gave His only Son, Jesus Christ, to take away our condemnation. By His work of salvation your soul is safe, a certainty that gives peace. He doesn't ask us to blend with Him or to merge into the infinite, but He has adopted us as His children. In Ephesians 1: 4–5 Paul spells this out:

> *In love he predestined us for adoption to himself as sons*
> *through Jesus Christ, according to the purpose of his will.*

God's original plan was for us to rule the earth with Him (Genesis 1:26), and through Jesus He restores this position to us. He takes our tears and gives us His love, so we no longer stumble along and blunder on but assume our rightful position in the Kingdom. On the third step, the view has changed. Inward peace is no longer about our story with

Him but about His story with us. We are no longer guided by our own "ego," but by Him.

Dance!

You are beloved and you are precious. You may have heard this before. So, what's so extraordinary about this? I can tell you from experience: The quieter you become, the more special God's great love for you becomes. As if you no longer listen with just your ears but with all of your heart. Every heart cries out for recognition. Everyone wants to be loved; each one of us is looking for love in all kinds of ways. I once read a story in a magazine that struck me. It's about a man who explained why he had a mistress. He tells us, "Seemingly, I have all I ever wanted at home: I have a big house, good food, plenty of luxury. But here, with this woman in her simple little apartment, for the first time I am truly happy. Here I am no longer judged, here I am beloved."

> Where are you looking for recognition?

This man sought love and recognition from another woman because at home he felt judged.

Jesus tells you He wants to give His love to you. He wants to change your status from judged to beloved, to turn your lament to a dance of joy:

> *Draw near to God,*
> *and he will draw near to you.*
> *Cleanse your hands, you sinners,*
> *and purify your hearts, you double-minded.*
> *Be wretched and mourn and weep.*
> *Let your laughter be turned to mourning and your joy to gloom.*
> *Humble yourselves before the Lord,*
> *and he will exalt you.*
>
> —James 4:8–10

> *You have turned for me my mourning into dancing;*
> *you have loosed my sackcloth*
> *and clothed me with gladness.*
>
> —Psalm 30:11

"Why walk when you can dance?" is one of my favorite mottos. Your garment of condemnation can be replaced by attire of love and joy. Your questions and troubles have not magically disappeared, but your heart is no longer cold.

> God is where I can come home, the silent presence and the deep understanding. This does not happen with the head or the mind, it is an experience; it is well, even though the world around you does not seem right at all. It is well—you are in connection with Him.[5]
>
> —Daniel van Santvoort, abbot of the
> Cistercians of Caldey Island

Is There a Fourth Step?

Well, that sounds great, doesn't it? From now on, you'll go dancing through life, with nothing more to wish for. And you'll live happily ever after. "Ever after" may apply here, as there is no time in eternity. But "happily"? It depends on what you mean by happiness. The Dutch Van Dale dictionary defines happiness as "a feeling or state of well-being and contentment, the feeling experienced when one's wishes are met." In reality, our well-being and contentment may be limited, and our wishes are not often met. And should this happiness fall into your hands, you need only to open a history book to realize that things can take a different turn. Or take a look around you. There are people living in your neighborhood who are burdened. Circumstances often rob you of the peace of the third step. You may remember intellectually that Jesus loves you, but your heart is worried, and you feel peace no more.

Shortly after the publication of my first book, a reader came to me. "Is there a fourth step?" she asked with a sigh. "A step where we experience a permanent state of peace without relapses?" The simplest answer seemed obvious: Yes, when we die and live with God forever. That's where permanent peace is. But that answer would be too easy. With that, we would deny the power of God's Spirit in our lives! It's true that life doesn't always feel like we are on the third step. In reality, as pilgrims, we go up and down the stairs, mining for peace and inward quietness. Some believers have had themselves locked up for years in order to reach this permanent state of peace. When I interviewed

Anselm Grün, he confessed with a half smile that he had written his book *Setting Boundaries* mostly for himself.

Let's be frank here: This is an ongoing struggle. But *how* do you wage such a struggle? Do you keep on stumbling on that second step, all by yourself, or are you assured of Jesus' presence by your side? The French priest and author Fr. Jacques Phillipe states the following about this topic: "A Christian joins the battle with a peaceful heart. He has the absolute certainty that the victory is already won. Inner peace is knowing that you are beloved, and that the Lord's mercy and grace are sufficient. This inward peace or mercy is a necessary condition to win a spiritual combat. But there is more: this peace is not only the *condition* for spiritual combat, it is often the *stake* as well. The devil does his utmost to banish peace from one's heart, because he knows that God abides in peace and it is in peace that He accomplishes great things."

Philippe also addresses the issue of *what* battle you are actually waging: "Our efforts should not be aimed at obtaining a victory over our weaknesses and sins. Jesus has already gained that victory. We must learn to maintain peace of heart under all circumstances, even in the case of defeat. Even though we fail and fall miserably, we should not panic. Get up again. And trust again in the grace of God."

As John 14:27 states:

Peace I leave with you;
my peace I give to you.
Not as the world gives do I give to you.
Let not your hearts be troubled,
neither let them be afraid.

If you have never tasted this peace, the text above merely contains words. But if you know the taste of peace, you know that these words contain a great promise. A promise that makes you go quiet. The clues in this book will help you to discover, practice, and keep this peace of heart. As Jacques Phillipe expresses aptly: "All reasons we have for losing our peace of heart are bad reasons."

INTERLUDE
MESSAGE IN A BOTTLE

In the following section, you will find a practical illustration that can serve as a reminder.

This "message in a bottle" teaches you the value of slowing down.

Quietude leads to more clarity regarding the truly important things in life.

Ingredients
1 glass bottle with a cap
1 scoop of sand
1 funnel or paper coffee filter

How to Proceed?
1. Put the sand in the bottle using the funnel or a paper coffee filter (cut a hole in it).
2. Then fill the bottle with water.

What Is the Message of This Bottle?

The bottle filling with water and sand symbolizes our life. When you shake it, the water will become muddy and it will be hard to see through. The same is true of our life: When we run and hurry and bump into everything, the water is splashing back and forth, and the vision becomes cloudy. It is difficult to have a clear view of reality.

Of course, you can buy all kinds of self-help books to read, but the message of the bottle is quite simple: If you just put it down quietly and leave it, the sand will settle, and the water will become clear again.

After only an hour or so you will see the water in the bottle is already quite clear. For crystal-clear water, you need to wait a couple of days! Leave the bottle on your desk, next to your laptop, as a reminder for some downtime or quietude in your life.

QUIETNESS FOR
NOT-SO-QUIET PEOPLE

Being quiet is easier for some people than for others. They simply love to retreat and quietly contemplate the affairs of life. They take part in the world around them at their own pace. At times they even feel like a nonentity. They watch others flashing by, fussing, and wonder whether they are missing out on things after all. I have a number of these quiet contemplators in my circle of friends. They are a relief to hang out with. Solid anchors in this turbulent world, people to calm down with. By the way, saying this doesn't mean I view the other group in a negative way. People who are not quiet by nature can be inspiring in other ways and can teach you about surrender and inward peace just as well.

> Quietude leads to clarity.

Challenge

I myself am quite the rambunctious type, having a way with words and always eager to take on anything. Enthusiasm is my number-one faith language. The language of quietude and contemplation scores well but does not rank first.

To be frank, even though I am a quietness trainer myself, I find it quite a challenge to include silence in my daily life. Being enthusiastic, I tend to wear my heart on my sleeve. Next thing I know, my life is filled with words and activities again. Work and bustle can be exhausting at times, but it is fun as well! And the things you consider fun are the things you don't want to let go of. The great thing is that silence has different facets. The forty suggestions in this book are not limited to the language of silence through seclusion. You can experience silence and quietude in many different ways. Becoming silent or quiet means making room. Room for God, for yourself, and for others. Room in which to breathe and live freely.

Quite a few people I interviewed on this topic are boisterous. Animated and exuberant people can be found in a monastery, and in the Bible as well. Remember Peter, always ready to say his bit. He is portrayed negatively at times, but that doesn't do him justice. In his excitement, Peter did walk on water! Peter often failed, but, just as often, God raised him up. Jesus Himself gave Peter his name, a name meaning "rock." A rock stands still and does not shake. You can hide in its shelter.

Surrender

Especially for not-so-quiet people, silence is crucial. They may discover they do not derive their identity from what they do, but from who they are. It's easy to get carried away by haste and hurrying. Before you know it, you are living your life controlled by clock time, jumping onto a moving train and leaving love behind on the platform. You may want something in a wrong way, no matter your good intentions. You wonder why things aren't going fast enough while being rushed, impatient, agitated, and edgy. Surrender to God is nowhere to be found. You can even be in a hurry in wanting to achieve inward peace.

> The peace of God is a "slow" peace.

In my personal process, I have discovered that the peace of God is a "slow" peace. It is a peace to practice in patience and to receive from God, which lingers much longer than an instant peace the world proposes to us. If you assume you can easily pocket your inward peace, you are fooling yourself. This reminds me of a quote from Anselm Grün: "Catching your breath to recover…takes a while." Not just a moment, but a while!

Pioneers and enthusiasts are often those who take initiatives for a better world. Their vigor regularly tempts them to jump the gun. As a counterbalance, we need quiet people with less vigor. Whoever forgets about silence:

- considers spreading love to be work. As if sharing the love of Jesus is an activity, rather than an obvious consequence of who you are.
- loses love. When it's actually about relationships based on love, instead of about organizing.
- runs ahead of God and will become frustrated and worn-out because God doesn't seem to be moving fast enough.
- thinks they can do it themselves and mainly rely on their own opinions.

- misses out on the amazement. Be aware: God is leading the way. He is in charge and uses you for His plan. Stop striving and start living.

I Am Already a Quiet Person

Maybe you are someone who already knows the concept of inner quiet in life really well. You may recognize many things from your everyday life in this book. That's really great. Make sure to share this quietude and silence; the world needs it badly! Don't judge the fast types in your life—doing so would rob you of your peace of mind.

Being quiet and calm doesn't automatically mean you possess an abundance of inner peace. You may be quiet because you are lonely—there's just no one around to talk to. Maybe you're sick and your circle of friends suddenly seems "nonexistent." For years, you have been bottling up all of your grief and you are sitting by yourself racking your brain over all that went wrong in your life. You may feel frustrated about all those boisterous people seemingly calling the shots. You feel like you're neglected, and deep within you wonder: Am I able to flourish? There's more, but I don't know how to get ahold of it. Only after spending three years in a cave did St. Benedict come to realize he needed others. Don't just sit there being left with all these questions, but share them with someone else. Get started with the suggestions from this book and don't be put off by those boisterous people around you! One of them may even long for your friendship. You can help and serve each other.

This book is a striking example of mutual service. I didn't write it alone, as I suffer from muscle problems. Maaike Bos recorded a large portion of the book that you are now reading. I am truly blessed with extraordinary friends, and Maaike is one of them. She is living according to the "slow life principle." She is quiet and takes time to contemplate life. She refers to herself as a little snail and calls me a busy bee. One day she decided to open up to me and refused to be impressed by my "busier" life. We opened our hearts to one another. Our lives differ in many ways, but in our hearts we are not really that different at all. We are both looking for recognition and love, and we are searching for God's way in all of this. Maaike and I have each experienced prosperity and adversity and, at times, we walk together like two pilgrims. We struck a deal. I have asked Maaike to tell me to calm down every once in a while. And she asked me to encourage her occasionally to show her talents, not to hide herself, but to step out in God's love. I thank God for this truly special friendship.

Pilgrim

For quiet and not-so-quiet people alike: You don't keep inward peace to yourself. You may enter the world with this peace, like Jesus did. For the sorrow of the people, He shared Himself. In a convent in Bruges, I came across a touching poem by a nun. A poem that says it all:

Pilgrim

A pilgrim I have been for so long.
I travel across plains
in the burning sun.
Through streets I roam
like a wandering guest.
Knock at peasants' doors,
sit down with the sages,
search with the deepest within

for the highest of heaven,
beg the Merciful
to deliver me
from the piercing void
in my anxious heart.
Here I am, I say,
but I am not really there.
Where art Thou, I ask,
but don't expect an answer.
Thus, I go, and I go
along lonely roads.
Thus, I hurl myself down
at the cloisters.
I sigh and I cry
till I drop down and sob:
I give in,
pick me up, take my tears,
put me where I must be.
I shall do what I must do

in the power of your breath,
for the sorrow of the people.

—Catharina Visser, nun and poet

WELCOME TO THE MONASTERY CELL

Some monks stay in their monastery cell for forty days in a row at times, to grow even more quiet and experience more of God's greatness. There they meditate on the Word of God. The word "meditate" gets on some people's nerves because it seems the equivalent of vagueness and fuzziness. "Meditate," however, simply means "to consider and to contemplate." This is not to be confused with Transcendental Meditation, a technique aiming to detach your mind from your body. As it happens, your body fully participates in all contemplations in the instructions presented in this book. These are encouragements to use all of your senses to experience silence. The word "meditation" is derived from the root *med-*, meaning "to take appropriate measures," which in turn is related to the ancient Greek word *medesthai*, "to care for." In silence you take appropriate measures to care for your restless heart, so it heals.

Modern retreatants prefer their own "silence cell" or sanctuary. During Lent, the forty days preceding Easter, and Advent, the four weeks preceding Christmas, they reflect on the life of Jesus and what He did for us. Many people do this by praying and fasting. Some fast by abstaining from social media; others fast by abstaining from food.

Practicable Silence

In the following pages, I present forty suggestions or Keys for silence. Hold on: don't shut this book yet, sighing and thinking forty days is way too long to spend on this topic. I want to share a doable idea with you. Author Wil Derkse interpreted *The Rule of St. Benedict* for novices. His book *The Rule of Benedict for Beginners: Spirituality for Daily Life* is a great success. Derkse is an oblate. An oblate is someone who is dedicated to a religious life, in this case Benedictine life, but has typically not taken full monastic vows. They take a monastic vow but lead a life in society outside of the monastery. Derkse's brother Geert, an oblate himself, taught him how to handle silence:

Half an hour of quiet time a day
One night of silence a week
One quiet day a month
One silent weekend a trimester
One quiet week a year

Don't be discouraged if the above seems too difficult to fit into your calendar. Something is better than nothing. Ideally, silence is to become a natural part of your life. You can do this simply by crossing out in your calendar this one night a week, one day a month, and so on.

And remember, when things go wrong, silence is nowhere to be found, and your heart is racing, just rise up and start anew. If you can't do it by yourself, do it together. No need to remain crestfallen as one who is condemned; rather, go looking for that garment of love and reconciliation. Don't panic if you cannot find it right away. The One who speaks through silence has enough time. Even better still: He *is* time.

How to Read the Keys

The danger of Keys is that they tend to become your next to-do list. As if you can lay hands on silence just like that, by reading this book. So don't try them all at once, but consider the instructions as instruments that will help you learn to walk in surrender. Like toddlers needing support when they take their first steps. Try the Keys and find out which method helps you to grow silent. Just "doing" silence doesn't get you to "being" silent. When learning to walk, trust and confidence are keywords, and the same applies here. Each Key can be practiced separately. I have ordered them in different categories.

Silence as a Basis

Keys that provide basic skills for your life. They take away restlessness and ensure that silence can become part of your daily life.

Silence in Motion

Keys for people who feel being in motion helps them concentrate. Silence can become part of your life like that.

Silence by Concentration and Contemplation

Keys that make you literally sit still. They can be really helpful to deepen your quiet time.

Silence Through a Change of Scenery

You can carry out most instructions where you live and work. However, sometimes it's great to get away and look at things from a different perspective or even somebody else's perspective.

PART 1

SILENCE AS A BASIS

KEY 1

A TIME FOR PRUNING

The air smells of freshly chopped timber. Dozens of pruned branches are ready to be inserted into the wood chipper. The trees look bare but tidy. It won't be long before they will grow buds again. But now they are at rest. Relieved of their heavy branches, they resemble fragile nudes full of promise.

Trees need to be pruned only once every three years. Many plants in the garden need a trim once or twice a year, depending on the level of meticulousness you strive for in your own yard; some people are fond of clean and tidy lines, whereas others fancy a jungle in their backyard.

Life is like a garden. All activities you plant in the soil of your existence grow and shoot up. If you never prune any of these activities, you will automatically end up with a lush, full garden. Before you know it, there's no spot left for sitting down to daydream or for growing something new. Plants, shrubs, and trees are growing everywhere, and the only way to move through your garden is by swinging from limb to limb. Seems fun for a while, but when there's never time to sit down quietly, you will grow weary.

GREEN FINGERS WEEK

In my own life I've had to learn that pruning time applies not only to natural flora. It applies to everything that has been planted in my life as well. At least once a year it's Green Fingers Week. That's when I write down which activities inhabit my garden of life and which plants need pruning. After that, I grab my trimming shears and set about rigorously. Pruning hurts, so I usually dislike doing it. When you prune the right way, your trimming shears will end up in living wood to enable new flowering. It is easier to lay a garden than to trim and prune it, that's for sure!

The first time my garden of life was rigorously pruned was when I was housebound by sickness for quite some time. Life itself got ahold of the pruning shears. I was used to my garden (I love jungles) and couldn't do much with that barren, arid soil that emerged after the pruning. For the first time, however, I was able to sit quietly on a bench. I sat there wondering what to do with this garden of mine, and that's when the Gardener walked in. He sat down next to me, and it was actually quiet for a long time. There was peace.

PRUNING PLAN

Do you dare to prune your garden of life so there will be room for the Gardener? And are there things that cannot flourish in your life because you prune too little? Maybe you are a pruner by nature. You know exactly when to drop your activities. When this doesn't come naturally, however, a pruning plan can help.

How to Draw Up a Pruning Plan

- Make a list of all your activities. Sleeping, eating meals, commuting, time to spend with your children, and social contacts are also part of this. After each activity, write down how many hours you spend on it per week and add up the hours. There are 168 hours in a week. On the bottom line you can see whether all your activities fit in one week.

- Make a list of priorities and write down how many hours a week you want to spend on them at a minimum. You can divide your list into Faith, Family, Work, Housekeeping, Sleeping, Relaxing (sports!), and other activities. You can include Silence as a separate entry, but you'd better include silence in all your activities. Account for space in your hours.

- Read Key 9 on Managing Your Time. Perhaps there's a lot to be gained by changing the way you manage your time.

- What doesn't fit within your hours and priorities is nominated to be pruned. Of course, you can rearrange your activities to keep as many as possible, but the question is whether that will pay off in the long run. Pruning hurts; there's no escape from this fact. "Kill your darlings" is a piece of advice commonly given to writers, the premise being "less is more."

Drawing up a pruning plan is a precise job. The way I outlined the practice above isn't necessarily your way. Allow yourself time to find out which way of pruning suits you.

> Do you dare to prune your garden of life?

KEY 2

STOP COMPARING

You are created uniquely, and there is a unique plan for your life. If you keep comparing yourself to others, you are like a tree that pulls its roots out of the soil to take a stroll. Wherever comparison comes, it draws the conclusion that you are just a drooping little tree. No wonder. Since this little tree hasn't given its roots the opportunity to ground and take root, it cannot grow into a flourishing specimen that is standing firmly in the wind.

DISCONTENT

Comparison creates restlessness and discontentment. These two are disastrous for quietude. We often compare ourselves to people who are better off in life, only to realize deep down in our hearts that this does not lead to a peaceful life. When you compare yourself to someone more privileged than you, you live your life in reaction to them. You may be fixated on the talents of that person to such an extent that you forget to develop your own talents and gifts.

Comparing yourself or your situation with people who are worse off can get in the way of true silence as well. A common assumption is that by comparing your situation with someone who has had less luck, you put things in perspective. But:

- Do you put things in perspective when you put yourself "higher" on the scale of (bad) luck?
- Do you take comfort from someone else's misfortune, rather than taking your grief to God to receive His comfort?
- Isn't this a way to downplay your own sorrow, so you don't have to think about it? Is there room for your sorrow?

It is best to look at someone else as an example of how to deal with a certain situation. And, while doing this, try not to fall into the trap of judging yourself or the other person. Why compare yourself to those who are better off or worse off than you? Stop it! Each time you are tempted to compare yourself to something or someone else, remember the following quote from Anselm Grün. In an interview, he told me:

> When you forbid yourself to compare yourself to others
> you will be in harmony with yourself
> and be content with the way you go.

KEY 3

BOUNDARIES

Following an interview I had with author and monk Anselm Grün, he showed me his study. His desk was covered with piles of letters from readers waiting to be answered. Requests for lectures were awaiting him. Grün pointed to shelves stocked with his books. "Pick one," he said as he gestured in their direction. It didn't take me long to find one. The book titled *Setting Boundaries* immediately drew my attention. Grün smiled as he straightened his habit. "Funny you pick this book of all the books. This is the one I actually wrote for myself."

Setting boundaries is a tricky business for many people, including well-known monks. You may not feel able to say no, and you may feel compelled to respond affirmatively to all requests from others, thinking you have to live up to all expectations. You may be afraid you won't belong or will be rejected. A problem with setting boundaries often stems from childhood events where others didn't respect your boundaries. If you want to live your own life rather than have your life lived for you, you will have to set boundaries.

COSTS

The concept of boundaries regularly occurs in the Bible. In his book, Grün cites the example of the Babylonians building a tower with its top in the heavens; they didn't take their human boundaries into account, for which they paid dearly. People who disregard their own boundaries bite off more than they can chew, building a tower that they can't afford. As Jesus puts it in Luke 14:28: "For which of you, desiring to build a tower, does not first sit down and count the cost, whether he has enough to complete it?" According to Grün, you could consider this a warning from Jesus not to build a bigger "life house" than befits your psyche. Getting to know your boundaries is discovering who you are, with all your opportunities and limitations. The trick (or the art) is to accept the latter.

BOUNDARIES AND QUIETUDE

When you start setting boundaries in your busy life, you will find there is more space for quietude. In turn, this silence will allow you to manage your boundaries in a different way. The reason it's difficult to say no often comes from muddy motives (remember the sandy water from the message in a bottle). Only too often you draw on the source of perfectionism, ambition, or your own needs for recognition or a rigid lifestyle. When all you care about is for people to notice you, you lose your boundaries. You will give yourself away. If you live from inner strength and draw on the source of the Holy Spirit who refreshes us and re-energizes us, you won't run out of energy.

This is such an amazing truth. If you take time to rest, you get to the Source, the source of everlasting love. And the great thing is that this love of Jesus then allows you to live fully within your boundaries. Through His love alone it is possible to love your enemies and perhaps even pray for them. Only through His love is it possible to overcome your fears.

DIFFICULT?

Finding it difficult to say no? The following ideas may help you:

- Saying no to one thing is saying yes to another. For example, not attending a meeting will give you time to spend with your family.
- Only by knowing where your own boundaries lie can you fight for peace.
- Always too quick to say yes to a request? Put a sign next to your computer saying: *Can I think about this?*

KEY 4

ALLOWING FOR SLOWING DOWN

One quote stayed with me from an interview with a Dutch politician. He explained how he traveled by train as much as possible. He didn't mind that this led to delays at times. His motto:

You need to include slowing down in your life.

A red light, a traffic jam, a tractor driving in front of you on a single-track road: Do you consider these things a nuisance or a blessing? Allowing for slowing down in your life is not hard; life itself already contains plenty of slowing down. The trick is to go along with it from time to time and to stop your own hurrying. Stress rarely solves anything. It's better to accept a delay and enjoy it than to let it put you off. So:

- Stop at red lights, even when you are walking.
- Allow for delays when drawing up your time schedule.
- Walk to the grocery store at your child's pace. (Make sure to take the afternoon off!)
- Dare to let go of your own plans to preserve some space for someone who longs for a talk with you. (Even Benedictine monastic plans and rhythms aren't "sacred" in themselves. Remember the story of the Good Samaritan, where the good man changed his agenda to help the weak.)
- Look out of your window and watch the hustle and bustle outside without being part of it.

KEY 5

NO MORE JUDGMENT

This may be the hardest silence Key to follow in this book. Judgment about yourself and others is often deeply embedded in your life. Judgment tends to keep you away from God, stemming as it does from thinking of ourselves: wretched and unworthy person that I am. Many an act is carried out based on judgment and condemnation: If I don't do this now, they will probably think I am a bad mother / employee / Christian. Anyone who believes in Jesus' redeeming work is acquitted from judgment and lives by grace. This grace is often under attack:

- *By ourselves:* When you keep dwelling on your shortcomings and talk yourself down, you press charges against yourself. You take God's judgment seat and pass judgment on yourself. That's called self-condemnation.

- *By Satan:* The devil just loves it when you condemn yourself. He confirms you in your opinion and presses charges against you if you haven't already done that yourself. In the Garden of Eden, he tried to talk up the human race—"You will be like God"—but now he runs us down. In addition, he ensures that you make use of the same method toward others.

The Bible calls on us not to judge. The only One to hand down a righteous judgment is God Himself. Please beware: This Key does not imply that, upon encountering injustice, you have to keep your mouth shut and sweep it under the rug. Out of love, you can confront someone with the consequences of inappropriate behavior. The judgment you should refrain from is the judgment that keeps you or the other from God and from the inner peace He wants to grant you.

> Some people keep on dragging
> themselves before the judgment seat
> of the merciless superego.
> They conduct a reign of terror
> over their own soul.
> —Anselm Grün[6]

TO RAISE YOUR AWARENESS

- Keep a tally and count how many times a day you express or think a negative opinion about *yourself*.
- On that same day, count how many times you express or think a negative opinion about *someone else*.
- Do the same when you blame your *circumstances* for failing to come out well and failing to lead you to experiencing peace.

AT THE END OF THE DAY

Be still and take all judgment to the foot of the cross. Ask Jesus to cast His righteous, forgiving, and loving eyes over this.

Repeat after Him and say it out loud: "It is finished!" Ask God to fill you with His love and peace.

WHAT IS THE NEED BEHIND YOUR JUDGMENT?

Often there is a deep need hidden behind our judgment. Are you mad at someone for not understanding you? Maybe you long for connection and acceptance. Do away with the judgment, but take your needs seriously. Make an open request to the other, expressing your needs without judging. People cannot meet all of your needs, so make them knowable to God. Leave it up to Him to fulfill your needs. He may fill your emptiness in surprising ways. For years now, I have been praying about my needs rather than my own solutions. This provides quietness, peace, and room between me and God. No longer does He need to meet the solutions in my mind; I simply offer Him my heart.

Sing this song in your quiet time:

Before the Throne of God Above

Before the throne of God above
I have a strong and perfect plea
A great High Priest whose name is love
Who ever lives and pleads for me
My name is graven on His hands
My name is written on His heart
I know that while in heav'n He stands
No tongue can bid me thence depart
No tongue can bid me thence depart

When Satan tempts me to despair
And tells me of the guilt within
Upward I look and see Him there
Who made an end to all my sin
Because the sinless Savior died
My sinful soul is counted free

For God the Just is satisfied
To look on Him and pardon me
To look on Him and pardon me

Behold Him there, the risen Lamb
My perfect, spotless Righteousness
The great unchangeable I AM
The King of glory and of grace
One with Himself, I cannot die
My soul is purchased by His blood
My life is hid with Christ on high
With Christ my Savior and my God
With Christ my Savior and my God

—Charitie Lees Bancroft and Vikki Cook

KEY 6

SILENCE WITH ALL OF
YOUR SENSES

Our bodies are constructed ingeniously, and God has given us senses to experience life to the fullest. We can see, hear, taste, smell, and feel. There is talk about a sixth sense: the sensitivity to observe and sense things outside our consciousness. This sixth sense is a popular topic for TV programs. Child whisperers and clairvoyants attract attention. This fascination with the sixth sense is odd. Why are we preoccupied with things going on outside our consciousness when we are not even using

> In quietness,
> our senses
> come to life.

what is within the reach of our consciousness? Together we pick up a whole lot more with our eyes, ears, mouth, nose, and skin than all these "clairvoyants" combined!

EXPERIENCE

Look at what happens when you grow quiet. Open your eyes and be aware of your surroundings and the people around you. Do they look happy, sad, scared, or angry? Are they withdrawn or in the center of attention? Ask God if you can watch through His eyes. You will see a lot more that way.

Listen to what is said when you keep your mouth closed. Other ideas or perspectives may surface. Perhaps the silence will remain. Suddenly a song or a verse from Scripture emerges.

Taste the salt of the sea on your lips, the cold of a Popsicle sliding down your gullet, the sun that turned your water into wine.

Smell new life sprouting up from the soil. The barren earth bursting open. The scents of a forest, fruits, and flowers. Be intoxicated by scents, just as God enjoyed the fragrant offerings people once made. Smell your own life. What do you think? Do you spread a pleasant fragrance that makes others want to know more about the Source you draw from?

Feel who you are in the depth of your bones—with all your ups and downs. Each feeling that can be felt is a signal of a human need. Identify those needs and discover that you are a beloved child of God. He takes your needs seriously.

REFINED

Feeling is a sense we tend to dismiss as "soft," but it is an intensely refined instrument. It consists of three somatic senses:

- tactile sense: the sense of touch;
- thermoception: sensing heat and cold;
- nociception: experiencing pain.

Jesus was very good at sensing. He didn't hesitate to touch people and even wash their feet. Nor was He afraid when people touched

Him—remember the woman with the alabaster vial of very costly perfume. He knew of warmth and cold by His stay in the desert. In experiencing pain, He is Master of us all. He asks of us to suffer with Him and to suffer with those who are struggling. Feeling is more than just physical. It evokes emotion and requires vulnerability. Discovering you are beloved is a basis to be vulnerable and to heal by sharing.

WASHING FEET

Try using all of your senses consciously this week. Take a walk, enjoy your meal, listen to others, follow your nose, and give a hug. Experience your pain, feel warmth and cold. Maybe you can even literally wash someone's feet.

KEY 7

THE ART OF QUITTING

I'm not done yet, but I'm going to stop anyway.

—FARMER JAN

Starting something is quite challenging for many people, but often the art of stopping is an even bigger problem. Just when you are doing a nice job, time's already catching up with you!

In a monastery, monks are not easily overtaken by time. They live on a fixed daily schedule, and when the chiming sounds they put down their work. Finished or not, they hurry to the service of God. Living in a daily routine gives them order and makes it possible to fulfill each task attentively. Putting down their work isn't something that comes easily to them, but they have learned that this discipline creates a focus in life. The silence and peace this produces enables them to spend time with God intently. There is a time for God, a time for fellowship, a time for yourself, a time for study, and a time for work.

This way you don't have to worry about balancing among the various activities. You don't have to wonder whether you will get around to certain activities, because there is a fixed time for everything in a day.

ART

How do you stop working when you're far from finished? You won't leave the meal you're cooking unfinished on the counter, right? And when you're in the middle of a phone call, you can't just suddenly cut it off, can you? Quitting is an art you have to learn. An art of discovering how much attentive work fits into an hour. Because we often want to do too many things at the same time, without a realistic schedule, our work is never finished. There are no impossible goals, only impossible time schedules. The tight daily program of monks may scare you:

> **There are no impossible goals, only impossible time schedules.**

you could do without such a straitjacket of inflexibility. This is no plea to ban flexibility from your life, but you should realize that the yoke of a hurried society can be more binding than a monk's daily rhythm. Just how flexible are you right now? Do you have any time to incorporate quietness into your schedule? Try using a fixed-day program to relieve your daily pressures.

- Draw up a realistic to-do list or set the goal of not completing your to-do list in one day.
- Set an alarm. Allow at least five to fifteen minutes of wrap-up time after the alarm rings. That way you have a moment to conclude the activity mentally as well. This may even spare you five minutes for a cup of coffee.

- Upon conclusion, think of what you're pleased about in the work you accomplished. Accept that you didn't finish it all. Plan a future time for the things you didn't finish.
- Tidy up the things from this task and then start another.

KEY 8

GET RID OF MULTITASKING!

We take pride in doing nearly everything at the same time. Personal life and work are mixed: with our phones we can send emails and tweets, use the Internet, and whatnot. "Wow, just look how many plates we can keep spinning at the same time!" Multitasking may seem effective, but in reality it is disappointing. Multitasking allows us to get sidetracked; we are constantly distracted and in the end the result lacks quality. Research shows that people who do only one thing at a time function much better. Heavy multitaskers have reduced memory and cannot retain information. The researchers suspect that by doing less, you can achieve more.

PUT YOUR SERVING TRAY ASIDE

Benedictines don't go in for multitasking; they believe every moment is worth paying full attention to. These moments have been given to you by God. Being really quiet to hear His voice is difficult when you're a multitasker. But listen, before you start judging yourself as a multi-tasker, first glance at Key 5. Then put your serving tray aside and sit at Jesus' feet, like a modern Martha next to Mary.

Multitasking is closely tied up with today's life. Here are some examples of how to stop multitasking from time to time:

- Give your full attention during a phone call. Some people keep on texting or sending tweets while talking to someone. That is disrespectful. If you suspect someone of doing this, ask them about it and explain that you would like their undivided attention. Some people think that being on the phone and cleaning simultaneously is an effective combination. Try to avoid that, too.

- Don't take your phone along everywhere. Why be available anytime, anywhere? People who can be reached at all times eventually become unreachable—their attention is running out.

- Are you watching TV while folding the laundry, or during a conversation with your son? Or perhaps as you are preparing for a Bible study? Effective though it may seem, try turning off that nuisance television and start paying attention to one thing at a time.

- From my personal experience: Sunday morning right after the church service can be such chaos. You have to fetch the children from the nursery, various people are addressing you with intense stories, you want to tell someone something about the sermon. When you get home and are finally having your coffee, you are drained from all that stimulus and feeling you have failed. My solution: I sit on a bench outside, in front of the church, and watch the churchgoers exiting the church building. When someone wants to talk to me, there is an empty spot right next to me, and they have my full attention. Minor things to arrange are done by email or a postcard. My husband and I agreed we would take turns watching the children.

- You resort to multitasking because you want to squeeze too many things into the same amount of time. Maybe you have too many tasks and you need to cut back. Glance back at Key 1 on Pruning.

- What multitask moments cause you stress, keeping you from quiet moments in your life? List them and look for a solution.

KEY 9

MANAGING YOUR TIME

One morning I was eager to start working. There would be no children around for three hours. There was a to-do list on my desk, and I intended to finish it all in the time ahead. I started the computer in good spirits. I lit a candle to indicate that I wanted to get started in a focused and attentive manner (see Key 29) and read the list. That looked realistic. I had intentionally put only one thing on it that was urgent and important, and the rest of it could be done at some other moment if necessary. Wow, what a good start to my day!

STRESS

Three hours later, I was completely stressed out. My list was not completed, not even the most important point. And now I had to ride like crazy to be in time to pick up my daughter from school. On my bike I suddenly wondered whether I had blown out the candle. Because I had not stopped working in time (see Key 7), I couldn't recall whether I had done it. Condemning myself and cursing myself, I careened back home. What a terrible fool I was! I'd ignored all the silence Keys from this book and wondered where things had gone wrong. The villain of the story was quickly to be found: that was me. Due to a choice at the start of my work process, my focus had completely disappeared. I had first opened Facebook and my email program and lingered there for two hours. All kinds of people were asking for my attention, and of course I wanted to have an empty in-box before starting my important task.

COVEY

Stephen R. Covey wrote a bestseller on time management titled *The 7 Habits of Highly Effective People*. The scenario I described previously would fall neatly into his matrix for determining the urgency of a given task. You can find Covey's time management on the Internet.

When I opened my mailbox, things popped up that were not important, but they felt urgent. That is to say, I felt I had to respond immediately. I spent most of my time doing that, like most other people (52 percent) do. Instead, I should have focused on the task that was important that I had already put on my own list.

What I Have Learned from My Own Trip-Up and from Covey's Time Management

- Put your to-do list in order of priorities.
- Start with priority number 1. These are often difficult jobs that require your attention. It's tempting to put them off, but don't do that. In reality, it turns out that you can complete them quite quickly, leaving you time for priority number 2.
- Take time for your most important priorities!
- Open your email only twice a day. At the start, arrange

---

your emails by priority. At the end of your day, decide which emails you can reply to the next day. In this way, you can prevent email traffic from interfering with your work schedule.

- Don't consider email a message to respond to, but as a task. If it takes less than two minutes to answer, do it right away. If it takes more time, turn it into a task and put it on your list.

Managing your time like this will bring peace and quietness in your life. I would have finished my task if I had put aside the non-urgent things. Then there would have been space to carefully blow out the candle and quietly bike to school, relishing the fact that I had been working on something with utmost concentration. Fortunately, every day grants you a new opportunity.

KEY 10

CHILDREN ARE LIKE MONASTERY BELLS

Wednesday afternoon: I promised my daughter that I would read her a book. She's ready, waiting on the couch. When I swiftly run upstairs to get my slippers, I see that the laundry still needs to be hung out. I can still do that quickly. There are things on the stairs that need to be moved into the attic. Then I remember I need to cancel the dentist, so I write that on a note. Suddenly my daughter is standing in front of me, highly indignant. "Mom, what are you doing? You are writing? That is not reading a book to me, is it? You're not listening at all to what I'm saying!"

Anyone with children in their house knows that silence is often hard to find. As a result, inner peace is often under pressure. Still, a home filled with children is the best exercise in finding and maintaining inner peace. Children are like monastery bells. As soon as one of them "sounds," you drop all work to pay attention to this situation. You happen to practice the art of stopping all day long.

> **Children teach you how to live in the here and now.**

Children sense unerringly when you don't give them your full attention. The example above shows that I have a very well-tuned monastery bell walking around my house! No more multitasking for me. I experience a day with my children as enervating, but I always feel that I am living in the here and now. The Benedictine daily rhythm of rest, cleanliness, and order fits seamlessly into a family. Just as there are pre-marriage courses, monasteries could offer a pre-children course to become an expert in peace, cleanliness, and regularity.

CRAZY

We may sometimes think that our children are driving us crazy, but too often it is we ourselves who create this situation. Working and having your child around you at the same time, while keeping peace and staying focused and paying attention…that's not possible. One of these will fall short. Of course, you do not always have to exclude a combination of work-and-child or housekeeping-and-child. Children may learn to play by themselves because their parents sometimes have other things to do. However, in today's society, more and more parents have other things to do, something I notice in my own family life as well. Do yourself and your kids a favor: consider them monastery bells that teach you to live in the here and now.

KEY 11

TAKING TIME TO REFLECT ON YOUR BODY

In everyday life we often make a distinction between our body and our mind. Our "being" thinks up all kinds of things to do, and the question is: Will our body be able to keep up with it all? Here's a practical representation exercise for awareness:

Place two chairs facing each other. Take a seat yourself in one chair and imagine your "body" taking a seat in the other chair. Ask your body how it is. Close your eyes and let your body tell you how it feels. Start with your toes, your lower legs, your upper legs, your stomach, your chest, your neck, your throat, your mouth, your nose, and work your way up to the top of your head. Are you suffering from cramps in your calves, stomachache, heart palpitation, stiff shoulders, headache, sore throat, a stuffed-up nose? Now, for a moment, park all those feelings on the chair facing you. And now tell your body with your mind what you usually tell yourself.

For example:

- *Sorry, but you gotta hang on for a while. Next week it will slow down.*
- *Have some painkillers—that will help you pull through.*
- *Quit the nagging. Just keep going; the work must be done.*
- *I really don't have time to be sick.*

Would you say this to a real person sitting across from you if they were dealing with the same complaints?

QUIETING DOWN PHYSICALLY

The first time someone did this exercise with me, I simply couldn't hold back my tears. By visualizing my body in front of me as a "person," I realized just how much I neglected and mistreated my body. My physical therapist said to me, "You walk all over yourself as if you are worthless. You ignore all stop signals. That's not a way to treat yourself, is it?"

From that moment on I started exercising (something I detest, really) and started paying closer attention to what I eat. For the first time I understood the remark of a psychotherapist I know. Her motto is: "If someone does not exercise, I won't treat them. You cannot work on your mental state while at the same time neglecting your body." I thought that was a fairly firm statement, and I increasingly see the truth of it. God created us with body, soul, and mind. If you work at spiritual silence in your life, you may also work at physical silence.

RUBBER BAND

During meditation, you can focus on your body by using a meditation stool or bench. This helps your body to sit in an easy and concentrated way, which will prevent you from dozing off while contemplating God's Word (see Key 23 for making such a bench yourself).

Sitting down occasionally in a concentrated position is not enough, however. When you lead a busy life, your body has to deal with stress regularly. Both positive and negative stress stir a process in your body that releases adrenaline, endorphins, and cortisol. Cortisol slows down the construction and maintenance of our body. It also inhibits the formation of antibodies. Your physical resistance is then decreased and most of your energy is mobilized to respond to ever-changing circumstances. Stress is not unhealthy as long as a period of recovery follows. If that period of recovery and slowing down is absent, you will destroy your muscle tissue. If you stretch a rubber band for too long, it will eventually lose its elasticity. With some rest, an occasional day at a spa, regular exercise, and good nutritional habits, you ensure that your rubber band does not snap and retains its flexibility.

- Exercise for at least thirty minutes every day and schedule your sports activities every week. Can't stand the gym? A brisk walk or a bike ride is good exercise as well.

- Create spa evenings in your own bathroom or visit a wellness retreat.
- Eat a healthy and varied diet.
- Watch your posture: very often you sit on your chair in an alert tense position. Try adopting a relaxed position more often.
- Learn to breathe properly—this is the basis of everything, and the next Key is dedicated to it.

The Bible compares your body to a temple. A temple in which God dwells. Take good care of it.

KEY 12

EXPERIENCING THE
FIRST STEP—RELIEF

On the first step of silence, we experience relief: we breathe again. It's as if we come to a standstill and sigh, "Peace at last!" The moment you stop, you will become aware of your own body. Pay attention to your breathing, which is affected by your moods. When you are afraid you take shallow breaths, and when you are relaxed you breathe more deeply. Breathing is a barometer of your emotional state and brings you back to the here and now. Deep breathing is much more restful and relaxes the muscles in your neck and shoulders.

A PRACTICAL BREATHING EXERCISE

- Sit quietly, for example on a meditation bench. Make sure you sit upright. You may also stand up.
- Make mental contact with your body by going through all body parts and checking how you feel about yourself.
- Put one hand on your chest and one on your stomach. Count the number of breaths per minute and feel whether you are breathing mainly from your chest or from your stomach.
- Try to breathe so you use only your stomach and the hand on your chest comes to rest (breathe toward the hand on your stomach). Inhale counting to four, then exhale for six seconds.
- When you breathe in, think of God's love—when you breathe out, let go of all deadweight and negative emotions.

- Do this exercise three times a day for a good balance in your breathing.

BREATH OF LIFE

The word "breath" occurs in the Bible more than once. God breathed the breath of life into Adam—His *ruach* into man. He rested on the seventh day, as we would say, to "catch His breath," (according to the Dutch translation of the Bible) to be refreshed (Exodus 31:17). On the seventh day, the rest was created from which we may face the world. In Exodus 23:12, God calls us to take a breathing space: "on the seventh day you shall rest."

KEY 13

EXPERIENCING THE
SECOND STEP—STUMBLING

In the eighties the American singer Pat Benatar scored a big hit with the song "Love Is a Battlefield."

If love is a battlefield, a war zone, as a human being, you may sometimes even feel that life is a battlefield, a war zone. You are attacked from all sides, in your sense of peace, your self-esteem, your principles, and your faith in God. The attacks come from the outside and from within.

Attacks from the outside are, for example, neighbors who disturb your peace, falsehoods that are spoken about you, or other incidents that happen to you. These are your circumstances.

Attacks from within are, for example, feelings of insecurity, mistrust, lust, stubbornness, pride, or low self-esteem. Under normal

> Don't fight against fear. Fight for love.

conditions, you may still be able to bypass these inner war zones, but as the conditions grow more difficult, the firing will start there as well. It's just like a real war: the enemy tries to find your weak spots and carries out the attack on them with precision.

ESCAPE?

On the second step of silence, the battlefields in our lives become visible. It's logical that you'd rather flee from them than face them. Fleeing from circumstances that make you stumble can be very smart, but it's not always possible. Running away from yourself is never smart; you're bound to meet yourself again sooner or later. You bring yourself along, no matter where you go. On the battlefield it becomes clear whether the message you have learned with your head has connected in your heart. Do you trust grace—or just your own fighting techniques? The words of God should move from your head to your heart. Quiet yourself and think about the question:

Do you trust your Commander-in-Chief? Do you trust Jesus' tactics and skills?

FIGHT FOR THE LOVE SITTING ON THE THRONE

Do you trust Him? That is the key question in the battle you have to fight. Do you believe that He means well by you, no matter your inward and outward circumstances? That vote of confidence has a lot to do with your own ego. You don't dare to surrender because other voices inside you shout the Commander's voice down. The voice of fear shouts that you may not survive. You have placed that voice on the throne in your heart, perhaps unintentionally.

Our ego is the biggest problem that stands in the way of peace. Jesus has come to wage war against your own "self." Let Him put off that ego. If you don't think you have an ego because you consider yourself useless, you are wrong. You put the voice that declares you useless on the throne, instead of God Himself. That is also a form of pride that has to disappear.

—Arie de Rover (in *Struck by Grace*)

These are analytical words that can be very beneficial. In psychology, the concept of "multiple part selves" is used instead of "ego." For example, if the "child in you" is damaged and is crying for attention, you can learn to acknowledge, recognize, and find healing from those feelings in the light of God's grace. It can be difficult to do this on your own, so don't hesitate to seek professional help.

How do you find out whether Jesus can be trusted? My experience is: Try walking with Him. The Bible is a powerful "walking book." Nature is also a place of learning to trust again; see the grass that shoots up even though it was mowed down? The closer you are with Jesus, the more comfortable you will be with Him. Just take that ego with its big mouth or that damaged child inside of you quietly to Him. You can rest there and experience what it is like to have a Commander-in-Chief who already has a hold on peace. He's smiling at you. You may rest assured of that. Grace is the undeserved smile of God.

PRACTICAL

- Write down where your outward battlefields are located. These are your circumstances.
- Then map out your inner war zone. Which thoughts and actions prevent you from trusting in Jesus? Pride, fear, or low self-esteem?
- In which situations in the battlefield above do you lose the battle?
- Fight to make room for love—first surrender these areas to grace and admit that you cannot make it on your own. I have learned this is where the healing starts. Do not get into useless battles that are both exhausting and unnecessary.

- Avoid places and circumstances where you cannot win the fight. If that is impossible, you have ended up in a challenging place in which you will discover a lot about your own boundaries, about grace, and about the verb "to love." This takes training, and sometimes you need help from others.

FRIEND

If you are your own worst enemy because you keep failing and condemning yourself, remember this:

The best way to defeat your enemy is to make him your friend.

The only way this can be done is through the love of Jesus. See yourself through His eyes and befriend yourself. If this doesn't work for you on your own, please make sure to find help.

KEY 14

EXPERIENCING THE THIRD STEP— PRAYING FOR LOVE

"You're the one for me," a man said. "Whatever you do or say, I know I want you by my side for the rest of my life." The woman could hardly believe it; other men had said this to her before, but they had abandoned her all the same. She tested him by being unkind to him, but he remained affectionate anyway. "I know what you're trying to do," he said, "but you won't be able to chase me off." The woman realized she had to take the plunge; she would have to trust him if she wanted to give this love a chance. After weighing the pros and cons, she decided to go for it.

Did you ever take the plunge? Would you dare to let God love you, or are you afraid that He will disappoint you? Deep within quietude you will discover with your heart and with all of your being that God loves you. You are beloved. Letting yourself be loved is an art because it requires vulnerability. Once you dare to be vulnerable, it is marvelous. You belong. Even more, someone else is happy because He sees you! Do you believe God is delighted when He sees you? Really glad? His heart beats for you; He feels a deep joy about you.

MEDICINE

During our Evenings of Silence, musician Ronald Koops gave a testimony about a special encounter in his life. Once, when he was interviewing a man, that man suddenly turned the tables and started asking questions himself. "Do you know anything about God's love?" he asked Ronald. And "How are you doing, actually?" At the end of the conversation, he told Ronald, "I advise you to take medicine three times a day, to regain balance in your life. Pray three times a day: 'Father God, show me how much You love me.'"

> Pray three times a day: "Father God, show me how much You love me."

I must have heard Ronald's testimony ten times before I dared to put it into practice myself. Just as Ronald had initially thought it was the strangest advice, it seemed odd to me to pray this prayer. Who was I to ask this from God? Nevertheless, I eventually started praying this, and, slowly but surely, something changed in my thinking. I felt more and more like a child asking for a hug—just like my own daughter sometimes does. And I discovered that God really wants to give me that hug. It was as if this prayer opened my eyes to His expressions of love all around me. I felt lighter and relieved. I felt like His beloved! I hope this medicine will help you, too.

KEY 15

CELEBRATING SUNDAY

So God blessed the seventh day and made it holy, because on
it God rested from all his work that he had done in creation.

—GENESIS 2:3

God blessed one day a week and made it holy, and He rested on that
day. Go figure: God Himself takes a rest from His work, when He is
the Source of all energy. He sets a limit to His work and gives Himself

space to enjoy and to rest. And not just a few minutes, but an entire day. When we hurtle on, on Sunday or any other day of the week that we have set aside, we are putting ourselves above God, so to speak.

WHY?

Why do we do that? What is urging us on when we want to continue our business on that one particular day of the week?

- The desire to control and organize everything and have it finished?
- The desire to make more money?
- The feeling of happiness that a day of work and being useful gives us?
- The desire not to let our boss down?

Quite often this is about our story, the one we want to convey through our work. Can we still really listen to His story and receive

Him at all? Our hearts are like a crowded inn in Bethlehem where there was no place for a pregnant woman. "It is fully occupied here with all kinds of important people who have already made a reservation or who came a little earlier. Alas, tough luck…"

May Jesus be born in your heart. Do you have a place to receive Him? Is there room to worship Him? Will a star in the sky stand out because you have time to look up instead of sitting bent over your work?

CELEBRATE!

Sunday is my favorite day. I say this from the bottom of my heart. Since we as a family have staked out our position with regard to this day, I can relax completely. This does not mean that we never have someone over, but there is no work to do. When my physical therapist recently asked me what really calms me down, I couldn't

> That's what God's rest can do to you: Before you know it, you are part of it.

help but answer: "Sundays! The one day that I can go to the house of God." My therapist became curious, and I suddenly had a chance to testify of God's peace. Unplanned. That's what God's rest can do to you: Before you know it, you are part of it. What wisdom from God to bless that seventh day. Let's celebrate it!

PART 2

SILENCE IN MOTION

KEY 16

START YOUR DECISION-MAKING FROM SILENCE

Sometimes life brings us major dilemmas that we must face. Should we do this or that in a certain situation and what decision would God actually require from us? We want to make the right choice and so we worry about it as if our lives depend on it. What if we're heading in the wrong direction? All this fretting obscures our mind. We hop from one option to another and ask all kinds of people for advice. Our minds become overcrowded with voices. Actually, we are like that shaken bottle of sand and water. The lesson this bottle teaches us is that of standing still. Slowing down brings clarity. Clarity provides insight. Insight can lead us to the right choice.

BENEDICTINE WORRYING

Worrying is unhealthy, and the Bible is very clear about this: Don't be anxious about tomorrow. The credo "fear not—no worries" is repeated throughout the Bible. Worrying originates from the fact that you have no control over a future situation. Indeed, you do not know what tomorrow will bring. That doesn't mean we shouldn't think about the future; the Bible also calls on us to calculate the costs before starting a major project.

So here are a few suggestions for Benedictine worrying:

- Pick a time of the day when you will think about your decision. You may very well take two days to make the decision. In any case, select a particular moment so that you are not tempted to worry about it at times when you cannot really pay attention to it because you are busy with something else.

- Ask a number of people for advice, people who know you well and who know different sides of you. Resist the temptation to discuss your dilemma with everyone.
- Make a list of all the pros and cons of each decision.
- Make use of a spiritual exercise that St. Ignatius of Loyola applied in his life. Live and daydream (so don't worry!) for a number of days about the one situation and then for a number of days about the other situation. Which of the two situations gives you peace?

Ignatius is the co-founder of the religious order the Society of Jesus (Jesuits). In an attempt to defend Spain against the French artillery in 1521, Ignatius's leg was shattered. He was bedridden for months. In the course of his convalescence, he experienced the love of God that completely changed his life. During his daydreams, he thought of chivalry and knighthood. This caused disquiet and unease. Then he would daydream about doing great things in service for Christ, in imitation of the saints. These daydreams left him feeling at peace and contented. From then on, Ignatius would follow this spiritual exercise in seeking his way.

- Become quiet and ask God to open your eyes to the right decision. If you don't feel that God is directing you, there may be reasons for that.

  A five-year-old boy asks his mother if he can play outside before dinner. His mother gives him permission. Fifteen years later, the boy calls his mother from his dorm room. He asks her, "Mom, can I still play Frisbee before dinner?"

  or

  Perhaps our dilemma is not a dilemma at all. All roads lead to Rome. Whichever way you choose, they can all lead to where God wants to make use of you. He gives you the freedom to choose.

- Restlessness may seem like a sign that you should not take a certain path, but that is not always the case.

To give an example from my own life: I felt very uneasy about our decision to live in a neighborhood where I initially felt unsafe. There were many people who did not understand our choice. The restlessness about this lasted for a long time. Yet deep down I knew that God wanted us in this area to spread His love. Every time I grew silent and went back to the Word, that inner conviction was there. The turmoil had everything to do with my own fear of letting go of my certainties. Always go back to the most important Counselor with each decision and allow yourself some time in quietude in which to find clarity.

KEY 17

WORKING YOUR GARDEN

He who plants a garden plants happiness.
—CHINESE INSPIRATIONAL QUOTE

Eighty percent of all Dutch households have a garden, but only 10 percent of the Dutch people enjoy gardening. People tend to put down tiles in their yards to avoid the inconvenience of maintenance. Certainly, you will have fewer weeds to keep in check, but at the same time it is a lost opportunity for slowing down and cultivating peace in your life. Research shows that gardening reduces stress. It lowers blood pressure and ensures a longer life. Children who as kindergartners are allowed to get dirty by playing outside and rooting up the earth are able to deal with problems and responsibilities more easily at a later age, according to Dutch research.

Active gardeners have a significantly lower level of the stress hormone cortisol in their saliva and have better concentration and mood. Seeing green has a calming effect. Sitting in a garden and allowing the environment to affect you makes people more resistant to the bad things in life.
—Dr. Agnes van den Berg and Dr. Mariëtte Custers,
Wageningen University

RULE OF LIFE

Gardens play an important role in monastic life. Monasteries often have well-maintained gardens and the residents try to eat homegrown food as much as possible. In his book *The Journey from Your Head to Your Heart*, Dutch TV host Leo Fijen, together with abbot Korneel Vermeiren, drew up ten rules of everyday life. It is striking that a large number of these rules are about the earth and your own nature. One of the rules:

You have to work or feel the soil once a week.

The earth gives you a sense of reality; it brings you back to your roots. You have been taken out of the ground and you will return to it. You can reconcile with your own nature by this contact with the earth. You learn who you are, but also who you are not. Anyone who works in the garden sees not only the unruliness of nature up close, but its beauty as well.

I remember very well the first time I ate a zucchini that I had grown myself. I was amazed to see how new fruits grew on the plant every day and realized: This is not due to my efforts, but these are graces from the Creator. Those who work the land know they depend on God and find quietude.

KEY 18

PRACTICING SILENCE
WITH CHILDREN

Every now and then we take a special bike ride with our daughters. We are not the ones to determine the route, but the girls can decide for themselves whether we turn right or left, based on their own intuition. Under the principle of "getting lost is discovering," we have arrived at the most special places this way. Getting lost in space, getting lost in time. (And at times it is very difficult to find our way back!)

CHILLING OUT

Planning for time to hang around or to be bored is an essential element of parenting. It stimulates concentration, learning skills, memory, creativity, emotional balance, inner harmony, and peace. Children are often just as busy as their parents. There are parties and activities at school, at the after-school care, with the family, in church. "Phew...I'm getting tired of all those parties,

> Getting lost is discovering.

Mom. Can't we just do nothing for a day," my daughter sighed the other day. Children really need that time for fiddling about.

AMAZEMENT

If you introduce children to peace and quiet, you will reap the harvest of it yourself. Children are highly receptive creatures; they live in close contact with their experience and are easily surprised. To live is to be surprised. When children talk about God, the most beautiful one-liners come forward. Almost as if they still live close to their origin. Elaborating on that, you can explain to your children the basics of many of the exercises in this book and set an example for them. When you take time for this, you will discover that it's often the other way around. Your children teach you things.

PRACTICAL

- Let children "mess about" in the garden. It's okay to get dirty!
- Spend regular time outside in nature and encourage children to look carefully at the things around them. What kinds of miracles take place in creation? Have them collect things related to all senses and together make a "sensory display."
- Let children light a candle in a church by themselves. Make it a sacred and quiet moment. Walk around the church and sit quietly in a pew. You can find beautiful old churches anywhere, and when you are away on a trip you can make it a habit to visit not just the local shops but a local church as well.

- Make them aware of their bodies. For example, what happens to your stomach if you snack a lot? Why is it good to know when to start eating and stop eating?
- Teach them the art of "being" instead of "doing." They are beloved. If they make a poor decision, they are not worthless themselves. So reward them not only when they do something good, but also when they relax or play happily. Reward their human *being* instead of just their human *doing*.
- Schedule an occasional "time-off afternoon." No watches or phones allowed.

KEY 19

FASTING

St. Benedict considered Lent a period of both inward and outward cleansing. You could think of it as a spring cleaning for body and soul. Fasting can be done in many different ways, but many practice abstaining from food and living on bread and water. This has a physical effect—your body gets rid of waste products—and also a spiritual effect. By not eating we become weak and we discover how much we depend on the sources of food God provides for us. We recognize we are earthly people and are confronted with our limitations.

Fasting can also be done in other ways. You could refrain from:

- alcohol
- social media/the Internet
- social obligations or contacts
- food you depend on, such as coffee or chocolate
- shopping and/or spending money
- domestic work
- radio and television

In the monastery of Anselm Grün, the week of fasting is combined with silence. During this period of silence, anything that was ever repressed can arise freely in the soul. We can "clean up" our inner selves without adding new rubbish. During Lent, you can rearrange your life. Grün gives the tip to clean out your own house and to consider what you could give away or put away. Do you really need everything that is inside your house? Which objects are blocking the tranquility or peace in your soul? Have the courage to give away whatever is redundant.

VOID

The course of fasting can be compared with the three steps of silence. You set about your intention in good spirits, but after a short while you become restless and grumpy. As you interrupt a certain habit, an emptiness arises—you have to learn to deal with that emptiness. The challenge is to fill this void in your life with God, to be filled with His love and His truth over your life, even at the most difficult moments. Only then will fasting become beneficial, and you may even be able to eliminate certain habits from your life for a longer period of time.

KEY 20

THE ART OF RECEIVING

In our achievement-oriented society, almost anything is feasible. We are in control of our own success. After listing your skills and talents, you draw up a step-by-step plan to achieve your dreams. Books on this topic often turn into bestsellers. Certainly, it is good to make plans, and we should make use of our talents. Focusing and setting goals prevents a lot of stress. Just don't forget the words *Deo volente* (God willing).

*Come now, you who say, "Today or tomorrow we will
go into such and such a town and spend a year there
and trade and make a profit"—yet you do not know
what tomorrow will bring. What is your life? For
you are a mist that appears for a little time and then
vanishes. Instead, you ought to say, "If the Lord wills,
we will live and do this or that."*

—James 4:13–15

If we want to grasp, organize, arrange, and control everything in our lives, sooner or later we will encounter the unruliness of our existence. It doesn't work out the way we want, or we get sick and we discover how small we are. We try to grasp it, but it dawns upon us that we cannot make it on our own with that concept. What we need is a new word to come to life: "trust." Trust in God's love and in His way with us. Trust is related to a receptive life. Do we want to grasp it all ourselves, or are we willing to receive?

AN EXERCISE IN RECEIVING

Go for a walk and look around you. Usually, our eyes seek the things we focus on. We approach the environment instead of letting the environment come toward us. Now slow down and walk at such a pace that things are coming your way, so to speak. Walk in responsiveness and trust that nature or the environment in which you walk may offer you something, just like that. Suddenly there is a mushroom, a tiny ant on the soil, or a small tree that you would have

> Slow down, become quiet; life has so much in it before we even "make" something of it.

otherwise passed without notice. You can also do this exercise with others and afterward share what you have "received." Ask God to open your eyes to what He offers you in your daily life.

Keys 21 and 39 are about other ways in which you can combine walking and silence.

KEY 21

WALKING MEDITATION

Walking meditation is a special form of becoming quiet. It is an easy way to bring spiritual enrichment to your daily life. In this form of walking, we are not focused on walking from A to B or on the environment (as in Key 20), but on the process of walking itself. Christian walking meditation brings you into contact with God and, as experts say, this skill must be acquired.

- Before walking, start with a short reading from the Bible or light a candle.
- Slowly start walking and become aware of the contact your feet make with the ground.
- Do not allow yourself to be distracted, but shift your attention to your feet, step by step.
- On the rhythm of your footsteps you can silently repeat a Biblical truth, just the way you might repeatedly sing a line from the hymn "In God Alone" written by the Taizé ecumenical community based in France. An example of such a line could be:

  My soul is at rest in God alone. My soul is at rest
  in God alone. My soul is at rest in God alone.

- Some psalms can be used well for this way of walking, since they have a certain rhythm and cadence. Psalm 136 is good to use, for example. See the first verse here:

  Give thanks to the LORD, for he is good,
  for his steadfast love endures forever.
  Give thanks to the God of gods,

> *for his steadfast love endures forever.*
> *Give thanks to the Lord of lords,*
> *for his steadfast love endures forever.*

- Start with five to ten minutes of focusing on your feet. When you practice this regularly, you will find that you can use this gait at any time of the day. This way, your footsteps literally tread on the way of truth and peace.

In the *Handbook of Christian Meditation*, Lex Boot encourages us to practice walking meditation in the church we attend. You can do this by yourself or in a group. Boot has learned that people who practice this look at the space in church differently, using the eyes of their heart. One woman indicated that at the celebration of the Lord's Supper, she would no longer just walk to the front to receive bread and wine. She has come to experience walking to the altar as a meaningful rite that is a complete part of the sacrament.

Keys 20 and 39 are also about walking and becoming quiet.

KEY 22

GET RID OF THE NEWS

On September 1, 2011, a Dutch newspaper I read published a remarkable article. It was not actually an article, but an essay, laid out in book form on the front page and the five following pages. Quite unique for a newspaper. The message was even more unique: in this essay, Swiss author and entrepreneur Rolf Dobelli argues in favor of canceling your newspaper subscription and putting a stop on news-gathering in your life. Never have I read an article in a newspaper that has stayed with me like this.

NEWS IS TOXIC

Stop reading the news, Dobelli tells us. News is to the mind what sugar is to the body. We find satisfaction in consuming news flashes. But those who refrain from news have less disruption, more time, less anxiety, deeper thoughts, and more insights. Some of Dobelli's arguments:

- *News misleads:* It focuses on what is visible and demands your attention for that. This is misleading because a lot of invisible things also happen. This way, terrorism is overrated and chronic stress is underrated.
- *News is irrelevant:* It usually entertains you for a short while, but it is not very substantive when it comes to the powers that really matter in your life. For that, you'd be better off reading books or in-depth articles instead.
- *News has no explanatory power:* It presents facts as a truth, and often says nothing about the process through which things came about. You could say that facts are more important than the process, the goal more important than the journey.

- *News is toxic to your body:* Panicky stories spur the release of a cascade of cortisol. Your body goes into a state of chronic stress.

- *News increases cognitive errors:* It looks for cheap explanations for events when some things cannot be explained and understood.

- *News inhibits thinking:* Short news pieces interrupt your concentration and affect your memory. News distraction is the greatest obstacle to clear thoughts.

- *News works like a drug and leads to multitasking:* You want to learn more and more about different subjects and ignore the parts of the brain that are necessary for accurate reading and concentrated thinking.

- *News wastes time:* The time needed to read the article, the time to regain your concentration, the time it takes to think about it during the day, cannot be restored or gotten back. Information is not a scarce commodity. But attention is.

- *News makes us passive:* It drains our energy and tires us. We adopt a worldview that is pessimistic, desensitized, sarcastic, and fatalistic. Passivity and learned helplessness are the fruits of information that cannot be influenced.

- *News kills creativity:* For true compassion and creativity, instead read a book or a good magazine. Choose the depth instead of the breadth, Dobelli urges us.

Give it a try: no news for forty days! Use the extra time as quiet time. Use the time to read a good book, one that exceeds the news and offers insights for every age.

KEY 23

BUILD YOUR OWN
MEDITATION BENCH

In today's society we are mainly busy using our heads. We often outsource heavy manual labor, and when we come home all sweaty it is not because we have toiled on the land. This used to be different. Due to our daily work, the body automatically got enough exercise. To alternate our main activities with physical exertion, here are the assembly instructions for a handmade meditation bench. You can purchase this in retreat centers or via the Internet as well, but it is a good exercise to make it yourself. When you have finished it, you can immediately sit on it to perform the exercises from Keys 27 and 28.

MATERIALS AND INSTRUCTIONS

- Seat: Saw a board of 40 cm by 20 cm, 2 cm in thickness.
- Side boards: Saw two boards of 20 cm by 18 cm, 2 cm. Saw a triangle-shaped piece of these boards of 3 cm by 20 cm.
- Place the seat board and the side boards at right angles and fasten them using three screws per board. The sloping side becomes the *bottom* of the bench.

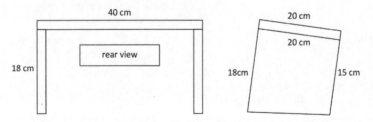

The board may be thicker, and the width of 20 cm may be 17 cm.

FOCUS

You lean forward when sitting on the bench. This will tilt your pelvis slightly forward. This position encourages sitting with your back straight. You get a concentrated, relaxed position so you do not fall asleep during moments of silence.

KEY 24

EMPTY YOUR HEAD
BY WRITING

The moment you sit still, it may feel like a relief (the first step), but soon after, the chaos (second step) sets in. Daily practice in silence can help you overcome the chaos. The following writing exercises can help you.

- Put your pen on the paper and write whatever comes to mind. Don't pay attention to spelling rules, capital letters, commas, and periods—just jot down what comes to mind. Write it all down, including the things you don't really want to think about or allow yourself to think about. Let your thoughts flow onto the paper without judgment until you are empty.

- It may happen that anger or rage toward someone or something surfaces as you are writing. Things you can't just put aside because they actually affect your whole life. Anger toward your partner because s/he doesn't take your feelings seriously. Disappointment that you are still not pregnant. Anger toward a manager who undermines your position time and again. Envy toward a classmate who always seems so happy-go-lucky. These can be battlefields in your life, to which you can respond with wisdom and tact. See Key 13, about identifying your war zones. For now, just write out your feelings. Ask God if He can explain to you what needs lie behind this and if He can help you with these battles.
- When you bear a grudge or anger against someone and you cannot make amends immediately, write this person a letter

stating clearly how his or her behavior makes you feel. Write down all your thoughts, including the things you would never really dare to say or that are unwise to say. Do not send this letter; just write it for yourself. Later on, there may still be a chance to discuss things, but bring your primary anger to God, naming your feelings in all honesty.

- Stay in this moment of silence and bring your writings to God's feet. Ask for His peace, love, justice, and blessing on all things written down. Destroy your writings after the moment of silence. Do not drag them along, but trust that they are in good hands with God.

KEY 25

FROM HEAD TO HANDS

The Norwegian fashion designers Arne and Carlos unleashed a new craze with their book *55 Christmas Balls to Knit*. They showed that knitting could be hip for men as well. And all of this is based on the principle that doing some knitting is totally relaxing. You can knit on your own or join a knitting group. Move action from your head to your hands to create space in your head. In doing this, you use a different part of your brain, which gives room for recovery. Did you know that taking this kind of rest actually makes you smarter? Knitting Christmas balls may be cool, but of course you don't do this year round (confession time: I myself really can't knit). Here are some other creative ways to "freeze" your head:

- Make a collage: collect inspirational quotes from books and magazines and pick up the glue stick.
- Start working with wood: learn to chop wood and don't freak out when your logs are not similar-sized.
- Take on a painting class.
- Search outside, in nature, for "treasures" that you can display creatively at home. This way, every walk becomes a memory to relish later when you are at home.
- Go out with your camera, focusing on the theme of quietness. Photograph what makes you feel quiet.
- Crafting is the rage. Have fun knitting, crocheting, or doing needlework.
- Start sculpting, carving, or take a creativity course in the community center.
- Bake your own bread and take time to cook your dinner

with careful attention. Buy products you still have to cut so that you use your hands to prepare your food with intentionality.

- Get yourself a real vegetable garden, either your own or in your community. Or clean up flowerbeds in your neighborhood instead.
- Take part in a writing workshop or start writing and drawing in your own diary. You can also start writing to a pen pal. For years now, I have been sending handwritten letters to a friend. Every holiday we send each other a letter, creating sacred moments in which to write and to read.

KEY 26

CONTEMPLATE BYGONE TIMES

God calls Himself "I am"; He is God of the here and now. In the Bible He reveals Himself as the God who has been and will be. He calls for remembrance: stories about His great deeds are passed on from generation to generation and people put up memorials that commemorate His loyalty. You can read about it in Joshua 4, when God leads the people of Israel across the river Jordan. The stones that were piled there, according to Joshua 4:9, are there "to this day." Becoming still and remembering God's great deeds are related. This is shown in Psalm 46, for instance:

Come, behold the works of the LORD. (verse 8)

"Be still, and know that I am God." (verse 10)

Apparently, you become silent when you see the great deeds of the Lord. Other translations use *cease striving* or *stop your fighting* (New American Standard; Holman Christian Standard Bible) instead of "be still," as if God were saying, "And now you stop it—first look at what I have done." To remember, we should pile those stones in our own lives. Otherwise there is a good chance that we will forget all He has already done in our lives. I keep a faith diary for my children. I record the things they now say or sing about God. I hope these will function as memorial stones later on in their faith life.

Some Ideas for Putting Up Memorial Stones and Reflecting on This

- Keep a diary of the highs and lows you experience with God. You can do this as a family and have several family members record in it.

- Record your prayers in a prayer journal. Look back regularly to realize which prayers God has already answered or perhaps answered very differently than you expected.

- Take time to create a photo album. You can look back gratefully on a beautiful holiday—time and space that God gave to you. Leaf through it regularly and reminisce.

- Remember your difficult moments, too. Was God present? What lesson did you learn in those moments? Those are insights that you may face again.

- Treat yourself to a beautiful piece of jewelry or a lasting gift on the occasion of something special. For example, the birth of a child, or your conversion, baptism, or return to God.

- You can also use memorial stones in the church. In a church I know, a stone is placed in the font at baptism. At confession, you will receive this stone with your name on it as a memorial.

- Immerse yourself in the history of the Jewish people. We believe in the God of Abraham, Isaac, and Jacob. You will get to know Him fully as you search for the memorials He has already left in the lives of these patriarchs. A visit to the Land of Israel is an enrichment. To me, the memory of the journey I took there is a memorial.

PART 3

SILENCE BY CONCENTRATION AND CONTEMPLATION

KEY 27

HAVING A MONASTERY CELL AT HOME

Monks sometimes stay in a silence cell for forty days to experience even more of God's presence. At first this may sound off-putting. Yet these silence retreats often provide a special experience and a renewed intimacy with God, as my interviews with experienced experts have brought up. In my novel *Shadow Flight*, Brother Daniel experiences such a period of forty days. I wanted to portray Brother Daniel credibly but saw no possibility of staying in a cell for forty days myself. On my way to an interview, I prayed to God for inspiration for this part of my novel. There was a quick answer to my prayer! The person I interviewed about his work as a manager stated at the end of our conversation that he would have wanted to become a monk. He once spent forty days in a silence cell and had a deep experience of God there. While telling me about it, he was touched by it again. I was allowed to use his experiences to bring Brother Daniel to life—that is when I became intrigued by this phenomenon.

FORTY-MINUTE MONASTERY CELL

Try to be really quiet for forty minutes, without music, phone, or clock.

This can be done anywhere in the house, but if things distract you too much, create an empty corner somewhere. Initially, all kinds of thoughts will bother you. Just let it happen and kindly try to get these thoughts out of the way. Key 24 can help you with this. It may be nice to light a candle (Key 29) and sit on a meditation bench (Key 23).

But none of this is necessary. Don't judge yourself for all the thoughts that come up. Let the silence do its work and see where you end up. The more you do this, the easier it will be.

Psalm 131:2 may help you concentrate:

> *But I have calmed and quieted my soul,*
> *like a weaned child with its mother;*
> *like a weaned child is my soul within me.*

KEY 28

LECTIO DIVINA

During retreats, Lectio Divina is often used to get Scripture across to you. Lectio Divina means "divine reading." You silently contemplate part of God's Word, following a few steps. You can read the Bible in different ways, and this way is about reading with your heart. So it is not a Bible study or a discussion of Bible texts. Although you can perform the Lectio Divina in a group, this reading is about your personal relationship with God. He can speak to you through just one word or one Scriptural passage. You can read how to perform a

Lectio Divina in my book *The Silence Diary*. There I offer 365 Lectio Divinas.

HOW TO DO A LECTIO DIVINA

- Choose a fixed time of the day when you take about twenty minutes to spend time with God.
- Before you start, light a candle to remind you that God is light and that you want to carefully seek Him.
- You can start and end with quiet music to calm you down.
- Read a Psalm or a Scriptural passage out loud. Do this attentively.
- Choose a text or word from this passage that appeals to you and keep it in mind. Consider the text in silence (for five minutes).
- Take your thoughts on the Scriptural passage to God in prayer and ask God for His perspective on this text. Be silent and listen.
- End with a blessing, song, or prayer.

SUMMARY

1. Consider the light—light up a candle, enter the light of God.

2. Consider your own heart—tell God honestly how you are doing.

3. Consider God's Word—read and contemplate: Which part affects you?

4. Consider God's call—what does God want to say to you? Let go of your own thoughts and listen to Him in silence.

5. Out of quietude back into the world—end with a prayer and go on your way refreshed.

KEY 29

THE CANDLE MOMENT

During a period of illness, I ended up seeing an elderly neurologist. He was unlike any other doctor I had visited already for my RSI symptoms. He took the time to listen to my story and to study my situation. In his home office he had a sideboard with candles he lit for his loved ones. When he told me a candle was burning there for me, too, I was deeply moved. A wavering flame was a symbol for sincere attention and hope for light at the end of the tunnel. I incorporated this in my novel *The*

Last Patient. The main character brings light back into the life of a broken woman.

LIGHT UP A CANDLE

- *Just before starting your quiet time.* As a sign that you want to listen carefully to God.
- *For yourself.* As a sign that you do not want to get ahead of yourself at this moment but want to bring to light your concerns, doubts, and restlessness.
- *For someone else.* As a sign that you are giving genuine attention to the other person and want to bring light to his or her situation.
- *For your plans in life.* As a sign that you want God's light to shine on your work.
- *To commemorate.* As a sign of hope when someone has passed away, or when it is someone's birthday.
- *For special times in the liturgical year or church year, such as Advent or Easter.* As a sign that a small light can change the whole world.

- *For an important moment of attention.* As a sign of sincere attention, you ignite a light. As long as the light is on, your attention is focused. When you finish the job or the conversation, blow out the candle.

You can light a candle almost anywhere: at home, in church, outside, in a cemetery, and even on the Internet. In Catholic churches you often have a beautiful candle corner where you can light a candle. Treat yourself to a candle moment every now and then.

> A wavering flame is a symbol of genuine attention and hope of light.

KEY 30

PRAYING IS TO BE SILENT

Many books have been written and read about prayer. This is not without reason. The Bible states that we must pray incessantly, and that seems like an impossible task in itself. We often feel guilty about our prayer life. Do we pray enough? Are our motives for praying honest and sincere?

St. Benedict included in his *Rules* a chapter on prayer titled "Reverence in Prayer." He advocates short and pure prayers. We are heard not due to a multitude of words, but because of the purity of our hearts.

He seems to be raising a major barricade: Who is pure of heart? Dutch journalist Rick Timmermans discussed this purity in his book *Craving for Peace*. He concludes that purity is not about sinning no more and being flawless. Purity is about longing for God. Do we long for God when we pray, or do we desire for our own wishes to be fulfilled? Father Helwig of St. Willibrord's Abbey in Doetinchem is quoted, stating:

> Prayer is to be quiet first of all. To listen. And you are not simply done with that. I am not in a higher state of exultation when I pray. Maybe at first, but that's not the point. The point is that you have to make way for God.[7]

AUTHENTIC

Benedict writes that our prayer should be short and pure; only by inspiration of divine grace it may sometimes be extended. This reminds me of a wonderful sermon I once heard from Hans Riphagen. This young theologian is a regular visitor of monasteries who became intrigued by the traditional formulaic prayers in the monastery. Form prayers are not that popular in our culture—it is better to say your own authentic prayer to God. Authenticity is part of postmodernism; it doesn't matter what choices you make as long as your choices are real. When you are authentic you have a story to share. It is important that you are authentic when you pray, but, according to Riphagen, we sometimes impose this authenticity on ourselves as a benchmark. The only good prayer would be the prayer that comes from deep within yourself and that you can express spontaneously to God.

Before you know it, this line of thought revolves around us instead of God. Every time you have to introspect and wonder: "Who am I at this moment, how do I feel right now, and what do I want to say to God?" This way of praying is very tiring, because when you are restless you cannot respond to these questions with an unambiguous answer. You will lose all courage to pray. A (short) formulaic prayer actually can help.

BREATHE IN

To pray is to become still. First listen to what God has to say. Jesus taught His disciples a beautiful form prayer that clearly expresses His will. The Lord's Prayer (Our Father) covers the entire Gospel. The

Didache (Teaching of the Twelve Apostles), an early Christian Scripture, recommends praying the prayer three times a day. We don't have to limit ourselves to praying only form prayers, but they can be a valuable addition to our personal prayer life. We breathe in and breathe out God's truth before we start talking ourselves.

Once upon a time there was a pilgrim who traveled all over Russia in search of a way to pray incessantly, until he came to a monk who told him, "Go back home and pray two thousand times: 'Jesus Christ, Son of God, have mercy on me.' If you've done that for a while, do it six thousand times, and if you can, do it twelve thousand times. By then prayer has become part of your breathing and you will find yourself praying all day long."

How to Include This in Your Prayer Life

- Pray the Lord's Prayer regularly.
- Repeat a phrase or a simple song in your head throughout the day.
- Use God's own Word in your prayer life. You can do this by using proclamation cards. Proclamation is speaking God's own words in faith, not as a spell, but in the belief that God's Word has power and never fails to work.
- Use formulaic prayers written by the Early Church Fathers.
- Make use of Taizé songs; these are little repetitive prayers.
- Listen consciously to the Votum at the start of the service. This is an example of a form prayer. *Our help is in the name of the* LORD, *who made heaven and earth* (Psalm 124:8).

The Shema is a Jewish prayer, which is pronounced at important moments:

> *"Hear, O Israel: The LORD our God, the LORD is one."*
> —Deuteronomy 6:4

> *"Love the LORD your God, and to serve him with all your heart and with all your soul."*
> —Deuteronomy 11:13

> *"You shall write them on the doorposts of your house and on your gates."*
> —Deuteronomy 6:9 and 11:20

Remember as you pray that Jesus Himself is praying for us all the time. We can rest in the knowledge that Jesus is praying for us, too.

KEY 31

CREATE YOUR OWN SANCTUARY

Anyone who furnishes their home dreams of a beautiful living room, bedroom, and study. All rooms and spaces are soon to be filled up. When thinking about the furnishings, you may want to include a quiet spot in the layout of your home. A place where you are not distracted by the daily worries of life. A place where you can light a candle, look at a crucifix, an icon, or a beautiful painting. A place where you can meet God undisturbed. Not having much space does not have to be a problem. Author and priest Henri Nouwen converted a wardrobe into a prayer closet in his room at Yale University. When he was in the closet, he was praying and could not be disturbed.

> I may have a thousand things to think about while sitting there, but the fact that I'm sitting there means I'm praying. I try my best to concentrate and not get distracted, but when after fifteen minutes I don't quite succeed, I say: "Lord, this was my prayer, however confusing it may be. Now I am going back into the world again."
>
> —Henri Nouwen

Give the candle (Key 29) and the meditation bench (Key 23) a prominent place in your own silence room.

KEY 32

SILENCE WHILE SITTING BACK IN YOUR EASY CHAIR

In recent years, a number of exceptional films have been released in which silence plays a prominent role. If you want to immerse yourself in peace and quietness, a film can help you to get into the atmosphere of stillness and internalization.

INTO GREAT SILENCE

This film is a very accurate representation of monastic life in its purest form. For three hours you will live with the monks in La Grande Chartreuse, the establishment of the legendary Carthusian Order in the French Alps. The Carthusian Order is an enclosed religious order that had never been filmed before. The life of the monks proceeds in complete silence; the film has no sound, either. There is no music, except for the songs in the monastery. There are no interviews and no commentary. You experience only the changing of time, the seasons, and the recurring elements of the day. By watching this film you imagine yourself in the monastery for three hours. With good reason a review called it a monument to slowing down and meditation.

INTO THE WILD

This film tells the true drama of a young athlete who, after he graduated from college, gave up everything to hitchhike and walk to Alaska and live in the wilderness. Christopher McCandless is twenty-two years old when he gives away all his belongings and sets off in search of the essence of life. He is fed up with materialism and a society focused on achievement and wants to experience the world how it was once intended, according to himself. He shuts himself off from humanity to live in nature by himself. The silence brings him to the heights of his experience but is ultimately fatal. When he gets sick and is stuck in the wilderness, no one can help him anymore. His story reads like the story of St. Benedict, who retired to a cave to experience true life. Eventually St. Benedict learned that God has given us as a people to each other; we cannot live in isolation.

OF GODS AND MEN (DES HOMMES ET DES DIEUX)

A wonderful film about the lives of eight French monks who live in harmony with their Muslim fellow-villagers in Algeria. The film depicts the final years of the community. Fundamentalist Islamic groups are increasingly taking over the area and requesting practical help from the brothers. The brothers are in constant conflict about this. Should they opt for the values of radical loyalty and love or should they flee? The story leads up to one night in 1996. On that night, the monks are taken from their beds and kidnapped. After two months, news of their death reaches the outside world: Their throats have been slit. Their intimacy with God enabled them to make choices that seemed humanly impossible.

QUAERERE DEUM (TO SEEK GOD)

This film is a documentary about the Monastery of St. Benedict in Italy.

In the Jubilee year 2000 the monks of Norcia breathed new life into the birthplace of St. Benedict. Armed with only their faith and their zeal, they founded a monastic community, which has been attracting men from all over the world to follow St. Benedict's ancient *Rule*. Many of their friends have long wanted an insight into the inner workings of their life, so they have produced this high-quality up-to-date film, which shows the monks as they go through the daily *ora et labora*. The title of the film, *Quaerere Deum*, *To Seek God*, reflects the true calling of all monks, the first and most essential quality of an authentic monastic vocation, as laid out in the *Rule* of our Holy Father St. Benedict.

THE MONASTERY

Five men searching for meaning in their lives accept a challenge from the Benedictine monks of Worth Abbey to live according to the monks' rules for forty days and nights.

NATURE DOCUMENTARIES SUCH AS *LIFE* AND *PLANET EARTH*

Watching a nature documentary may not have much to do with a monastery, but it does have everything to do with silence. Anyone looking at the stunning images of creation can only marvel breathlessly at so much beauty. "Mom, did God really make all of this?" my five-year-old daughter asked as we watched a documentary together. And when I answered in the affirmative, she sighed: "Phew, this makes me completely silent."

KEY 33

EATING IN SILENCE

I wrote a large part of my first novel in the Achelse Kluis. This is a silence monastery where meals are enjoyed in silence. *Eat in silence* is written on the small wooden signs at each table. Never before have I eaten such delicious potato soup. I tasted the dry bread extra well, and the rich taste of the dark brewed monastery beer was fully appreciated. Eating in silence makes you aware of what you eat and where it comes from. You can also try this at home.

A BRIEF INSTRUCTION FOR EATING IN SILENCE

- Choose a place where you can eat really quietly—not in front of the TV.
- Take a good look at your food before putting it in your mouth. Find out what it is made of and where it comes from. Ask for a blessing over the food.
- Notice how hungry you are.
- Taste a bite and consider what the taste sensation does to you.
- Try not to gobble down the food, but pay attention to every bite. When your plate is empty, consider whether you have had enough in relation to the hunger or appetite you felt at the beginning. Based on that, you make a conscious decision to stop eating or to scoop up another plateful. Mindful eating can help you in the search for a healthy diet. We often wolf down everything out of habit.

- With small children at your dinner table, the above seems like a fairy tale. Try it out with them nonetheless, if only for dessert. Turn it into a fun game.

DIETARY LAWS

By eating in silence, you reflect on your food. Dutch people are not used to this, but in many cultures food is linked to religion. Think about Muslims with their rituals around meals. Food plays an important role in the Bible. In the Old Testament the Jewish people had to adhere to all kinds of dietary laws that referred to God's faithfulness, for example, during the exodus from Egypt. Anyone studying the dietary laws will see that God has given thought to what we should and should not eat and what is healthy for us. And although we no longer fall under judgment of this law with Jesus' coming, the concerns are still very beneficial.

Eating silently is one way to reflect on your food, but such reflection can also be done in other ways:

- Study the dietary laws and learn what God meant by them. There are various publications in print. Ask for them in your local bookstore.
- Consider the sustainability of your own food consumption. Is the way you consume "fair," or do other people have to pay the price for it?
- Turn your meal into an attentive feast that will make you lick your fingers. You can use all your senses while eating. Eat at a carefully set table.

PART 4

SILENCE THROUGH A CHANGE OF SCENERY

KEY 34

HEADING OUT FOR A RETREAT

It is necessary to create silence and quietude in the place where you live and work. Then again, it can be so inspiring to go out every now and then, in search of silence. A different environment can help you let go of it all. There are countless options for short and long retreats. Below you will find a small selection.

LONG PERIOD OF TIME

- Go on a pilgrimage to the city of Santiago de Compostela in Spain and walk the Camino de Santiago (the Way of Saint James). Many pilgrims have preceded you. You will find lots of information on the Internet. Have a look at the following site: http://santiago-compostela.net/, for instance.

- Visit an abbey, a monastery, or a retreat center for a few days. The number of monastic visits has increased significantly in recent years. I organize retreats myself; many people enjoy spiritual guidance. Find out whether you can arrange a conversation with a resident in the monastery or convent where you are staying. This is often the case.

- Book a holiday home yourself for a couple of days and stay there by yourself. Bring some good books, a diary, and hiking shoes. Face any reservations that you may have about being alone and know that you are *not* alone. Jesus likes to go with you, just like your angels do. You will be amazed at the effect such a time-out will have on your soul. My husband and I take turns going out like this twice a year.

SHORT PERIOD OF TIME

- You can go on smaller pilgrimages in scenic areas near your own residence. Walk a pilgrimage route or choose a nice walking route.

- Visit a museum and take a seat in front of a painting for a longer time. This will provide you with different perspectives.

- Go for a night of wilderness camping in nature. You get away from it all. You can even do this between two working days. Bring a tent and look for a getaway. One night works wonders.

- Choose a three-square-foot spot in your garden and sit there for an hour. Discover what is going on in this three-square-foot area. Feel what it does to you when you are limited from the outside. Will you manage to make the journey inside? What emotions do you experience? Many people cannot sit still because of assumptions and experiences with silence in their childhood. The square-meter exercise often brings out a lot of frustration, but it leads to a lot of insight as well.

KEY 35

CONSIDER THE OTHER

Consider the other person. At first this may seem like an activist appeal instead of an idea for reflection and peace. You may ask: Do I have to be ready to help the other person? Can't I just sit quietly on the couch for a short while to deal with my own restless heart? To us, taking time for someone else means we have to do all kinds of things. We have to help the other with a problem; we have to be of importance to the other. And we tend to forget that focusing on the other can mean receiving from the other and receiving the other as a gift.

I incorporated a good example of this in my novel *The Last Patient*. In it I described a meeting with an elderly neurologist—a meeting that took place in my own life. My neurologist had examined many patients in his life. Now he was old and lived in a retirement home. He suffered from loneliness and longed for people to

> Considering the other is receiving from and of the other. See the other as a gift—you can learn to rest together.

have meaningful conversations with. A special relationship developed between us. While I listened to his stories about his past, he gave me a piece of his zest for life. I had lost it myself during a period of illness. We also met apart from the consultations, and I began to reflect on his life. I was surprised by the insights and wisdom he taught me; I received from him. He gave me his being as a gift.

AN EMPTY DINNER TABLE
AT CHRISTMAS

Elderly people can teach us a lot about dealing with silence. They are often forgotten in our society, while they really have a lot of wisdom to offer. Try to consider the elderly people in your neighborhood. I heard about an elderly man who wanted to share something with those around him. He organized a Christmas dinner and invited a large number of congregation members. This is how he wanted to show his involvement. Nobody accepted the invitation. His hands were full, but there were no open hands to receive his attention. He's not the only one. An eighty-five-year-old woman sent me a letter in response to an article I wrote on loneliness. This letter was not a lament, but a call for reflection. She included this note she had written herself.

> *We are so busy!*
> *What is so important in our life?*
> *We are looking for peace and quietness.*
> *There is so much turmoil to be found,*
> *and that is often at the expense of happiness!*

It is a time of hurrying and speeding up;
there is lots to do for many a one.
Can all this toiling be sustained?
Where should we turn to with all our hastening?
Take some time to contemplate—
and listen to the Lord—live by His commandment.
Then we will gladly perceive
what is important in our life: the rest in God.

      —Mrs. Van de Z., eighty-five years old

KEY 36

VISIT A LABYRINTH

You can visit labyrinths in different places all over the country. Many people confuse a labyrinth with a maze, but there is quite a difference between the two. A maze is a wandering garden in which you get lost, and a labyrinth is set up in such a way that you will *find* your way. There is only one path, and whoever walks that path will eventually reach the end point. A labyrinth is said to reflect the path of life; it is an ancient symbol for the search for our inner source and for what really drives us. Anyone walking a labyrinth may be surprised by the twists and turns in the path. The art is simply to keep walking, to continue, to live life. When walking a labyrinth, the journey is equally as important as the destination itself.

KNEELING DOWN

You come across labyrinths everywhere. In medieval churches, the symbol was sometimes incorporated into the paving stones and one was intended to take this path while kneeling. You may find a finger labyrinth at the entrance of some Orthodox monasteries. You can "walk" this labyrinth with your hand. Labyrinths can also be found at monasteries. Search the Internet to find different options for labyrinths to visit near you.

Points to Consider when Walking a Labyrinth

- Walk consciously and attentively.
- The outward journey is about letting go: free your mind from everyday things.
- Staying in the center is about receiving: take rest and open your mind to insights.
- On the way back, you make yourself familiar with what you have received: prepare your plans based on your new insights. You approach life receptively.

The symbol of the labyrinth can also be found in a statement that Jesus made about Himself.

He compares Himself to the door to life. You will be saved if you walk in through Him, the door. Jesus invites you to walk in and out again. His literal words are: "If anyone enters by me, he will be saved and will go in and out and find pasture" (John 10:9). This invitation is visible in the labyrinth.

KEY 37

TASTE THE SILENCE— HAVE A BEER

Ever wondered what silence tastes like? Here are some qualifications from a monk from Koningshoeven Abbey:

> Fruity, bittersweet, light and aromatic, fresh-hoppy, matured, mild, and pleasant.

How does that sound? To actually experience all these flavors, you have to taste their six different Trappist beers, the only beer in the Netherlands that can bear this name. They advertise their beers with the phrase "Taste the silence." They are right. What could be better than enjoying the peace and quiet over a dark craft beer?

TRAPPIST ABBEY

The nice thing is that you can combine tasting these beers with a visit to the Trappist abbey. Stay in the guesthouse and enjoy a conversation with one of the monastery residents. Trappist beer is brewed in other parts of Europe as well.

The seven original Trappist breweries are:

- Abbey of St. Benedict (Achelse Kluis) in Achel (Belgium)
- Scourmont Abbey in Chimay (Belgium)
- Rochefort Abbey in Rochefort (Belgium)
- Westmalle Abbey in Westmalle (Belgium)
- Abbey of St. Sixtus in Westvleteren (Belgium)

- Orval Abbey in Villers-devant-Orval (Belgium)
- Mont-des-Cats Abbey in Godewaersvelde (France)

ENJOY GRATEFULLY

Don't like beer? Drinking and eating your food mindfully also gives a sense of quietude. Take your time to learn about the preparation method and the background of your food.

Our lives changed drastically when we as a family decided to try to live plastic free. Since then, we have been obtaining our food from the farmer more often—we learned more about different types of vegetables and their growing seasons. Our food and drink is surrounded by much more gratitude ever since.

KEY 38

INTRODUCE SILENCE IN YOUR CONGREGATION

In the preface to this book, I told you about judo champion Dennis van der Geest. The greatest thing that could happen to him was to find inner peace. He is not the only Dutch celebrity to realize that peace and quiet is worth more than having a lot of money in your bank account. In a TV interview, Dutch actress, singer, and TV personality Katja Schuurman talked about her search for inner peace. She explained how Zen meditation and silence had brought her to where she wanted to be. For the first time, she felt truly happy and loved. In the past she had taken on too much in her own craving for recognition. It was a truly moving interview.

HOLE

Would Katja have been able to find the same kind of peace in church? Are we, as a church, good ambassadors of the peace that Jesus wants to give? To make this hit home for you, I ask: Are you, as a Christian, an ambassador of Jesus' peace? I fear that we as a church and as Christians have been dropping a few stitches here—so many stitches that a hole has opened up. We are very good at *doing* good deeds, and in church we don't often sit still. The truth is often preached with words. Where is the peace and tranquility we yearn for? Why is the concept of quietude mainly linked to the Eastern religions, while it has Christian roots as well? Peace and stillness bring the Gospel deep into our hearts.

AMBASSADORS

Let us be ambassadors of peace by putting silence and quietude on the agenda in our churches. Here are some suggestions:

- Take time together to start the church service attentively. Consider your body, sit down with concentration, shake hands with your neighbor, light a candle, have a moment of silent prayer together. In short, create a moment of peace and space that evokes expectation. God will soon be speaking—and you will be on the edge of your seat!
- Introduce a moment of silence after the meditation.
- Listen to quiet songs or music.
- Ask your pastor to make the silent prayer last longer than fifteen seconds.
- Set up a quiet room to visit after the service.
- Organize an evening of silence and quietude in your congregation.
- Consider each other as church members. Take the time to listen to the story of a brother or sister you do not have much contact with. God shows Himself in life stories; you just have to make room to receive those stories (see also Key 35).
- Organize a craft meeting on this topic and hang the artworks in church.

KEY 39

SILENCE WALK IN NATURE

> If one just keeps on walking, everything will be all
> right.
>
> —SØREN KIERKEGAARD

Walking is a tried and tested way to calm down. Walking is used as a means in social work and therapy as well, to bring people to understanding. And, furthermore, what could be better than walking around in God's creation? In nature, lessons for life are all over the place. We seem to have forgotten how to walk in peace. Walking has become a functional way of getting from A to B. We forget that the journey can be an end in itself. To quote a monk I once spoke with:

> The most important thing about walking is walking itself, not reaching your destination. Every footstep is life, every footstep is peace. That's why we don't have to hurry and why we take slow steps.

RELAX

The goal is not the end, but the journey itself, living in the here and now. The great thing is that as a believer traveling in the here and now, you may understand that the ultimate goal has already been achieved. As a Christian, you do not walk from A to B, but you start from B. You start with the goal: a loving God. He has already achieved the goal for us, saying, "It is finished." So, filled with His love, you walk your life's path. How does that sound? Quite relaxing, I'd say.

PILGRIMAGE IN NATURE

Nature gives us many tools that help us to live in freedom and with inner peace. I have been guiding silence walks for years in which we practice silence lessons in relation to nature. During these walks we use all our senses, and nature shares its life lessons with us.

EXAMPLES FROM NATURE

How much "germinative power" do you have? You tend to see what is in front of you. You admire a flowering plant for its beauty. A large tree is awe-inspiring. But what about the sprouting capacity of a tiny little plant you barely notice? Maybe in thirty years it will have grown into a tree with branches in which birds can nest, but right now you pass it by. How much value do you attach to the small things in your life? Do you also respect the budding power that God has placed in you?

> When we are earthed, connected to creation and its Creator, we can truly live in peace.

In creation there is room for

seasons. Plants come to life; plants die. In the woods, you come across mighty trees—fallen down as if they have stumbled in the middle of their existence never to get up again. They rot and seem to have no function anymore. A "stumbled" tree can remind us of the stumbling in our own life. To what extent do you dare to consider the seasons in your life? Is there room for grief, failing, and falling short on the one hand and room for life, joy, and celebration on the other?

What kind of tree are you? When you walk around in the woods you will see many different trees. One has a bare crown, another a full one. On some, the tops reach far into the sky, while others let their branches hang. There can be several reasons for this; one tree is exposed to wind to a greater degree than others, or one has been shaded by a larger tree. Psalm 1 compares a man who takes delight in the law of the Lord to a tree: A tree planted by streams of water, yielding its fruit in its season, whose leaf does not wither, and in all he does, he prospers. Do you believe in this promise when you feel merely like a skinny, tiny birch trunk? Just spread out your branches to heaven with expectation, like trees do.

KEY 40

COPY THE ART OF
A NATURAL

On an ordinary Sunday morning, I suddenly noticed her: a radiant woman, dressed in plain clothes. I observed how she enjoyed the service with all her senses and that she was perfectly happy with her God. I did not know her life story, but I could tell that she had already been through a lot. The lines around her eyes, a tooth missing. She did not look rich in a material sense, but never before had I met a woman who owned so much. "Peace"—that was the word I thought of when I looked at her. The next Sunday, I sat close to her and the sight of her alone made me happy. Her enthusiasm for God, her surrender, and her responsiveness were contagious. She sat in the same place every Sunday.

BEST-DRESSED

Apparently, I wasn't the only one who noticed her. She was interviewed for a women's magazine. For the occasion, they had her put on makeup and dressed her in something I'd never seen her wear before. Actually, I thought it was too bad; she didn't have to be made any "prettier." I read her life story for the first time and I was touched by it. She had been through a lot more than I had thought. But her circumstances hadn't gotten her down. She found God and, with that, she obtained the greatest treasure a person can possibly possess. Irina, you may have recognized yourself in this story. Thanks for being there! I enjoy you and know I can learn a lot from you, about the peace that hangs around you like a beautiful cloak. You may not have much money for new clothes, but to me you are one of the best-dressed women I know.

CRISIS

There are other people like Irina. Throughout history, we can find beautiful examples of people who shared peace. This makes me think of Mother Teresa or Father Damien. Their lives have been documented in writing and made into movies, and these stories are inspiring to read or watch. I have had the privilege of interviewing such persons of peace. I think of an elderly Israeli man who survived more than eleven concentration camps. Isaac Goldfinger did not become embittered but testified of God's love to many. Or a man who became paralyzed and who experienced the peace of God so deeply he testifies about it everywhere. And how about a woman who continues to love her husband despite his addiction to porn?

It is striking that almost all of these people have experienced a crisis in their lives. They stumbled, but got up, stronger than ever. Not on their own strength, because they no longer had it. Someone showed me a book in which the author claims that God always wants to bless you, also in a material sense. The author's reasoning: How can you be a blessing to others if you don't have money or health yourself? That's an understandable question, but I cannot agree with the reply that God wants to give you everything for that reason. God does not depend on people's circumstances. He shows His strength, especially in weak people. They often have nothing left in their lives except empty hands.

It is easier to receive with empty hands than with full hands. This is not always true—let's be honest about that. Sometimes you feel empty and weak and your sorrow and pain get in the way, leaving no room to receive. You have stumbled and never seem to get up again. Become quiet. Pray for God's grace that you will be able to live within His love. For some people, this takes a very long time and may require therapy. There are people who take their own lives because it took too long for them. Which is terribly difficult to understand. Why do some people suffer so much, yet are still unable to rise above their circumstances? Why is this given to some and not to others? These are questions that make you fall silent.

COPYING

People like Irina help me. They don't answer all my questions, but they do teach me to live without trying to understand everything. Do you know someone like that you can "copy" in your own life? The pitfall here is you may start comparing yourself with the other. You don't have to; just read Key 2. You can learn from the other. After all, that's how we all started learning things as children: watching somebody do a task and then trying to do it ourselves.

So don't surround yourself only with fast and restless types, but also with people who have a slightly different attitude toward life. Meet up with natural talents of peace and quietude and serve each other. When you are a natural yourself, share it! Take the other person by the hand and be a walking cane for your fellow pilgrim. Because:

> *We are pilgrims on a journey.*
> *We are brothers on the road.*
> *We are here to help each other*
> *Walk the mile and bear the load.*
> *I will hold the Christ-light for you*
> *In the night time of your fear.*
> *I will hold my hand out to you;*
> *Speak the peace you long to hear.*
>
> —"The Servant Song," Richard Gillard
> and Betty C. Pulkingham

CONCLUSION

We are on a journey together.

The forty suggestions in this book are meant for sharing. When we share them, we are connecting with one another.

Wishing you blessings on your personal pilgrimage—I hope we will meet again someway.

Never forget that silence starts with grace. Use those forty Keys as playing materials to discover the love that is already there for you. You are a beloved one!

NOTES

1. L. Fijen, *De reis van je hoofd naar je hart* (Kampen: Ten Have, 2007), 45.

2. A. Grün, *De mooiste wijze teksten van Anselm Grün* (Kampen: Ten Have, 2007), 59.

3. A. Grün, *De mooiste wijze teksten van Anselm Grün* (Kampen: Ten Have, 2007), 47.

4. L. Fijen, *De reis van je hoofd naar je hart* (Kampen: Ten Have, 2007), 46.

5. L. Fijen, *De reis van je hoofd naar je hart* (Kampen: Ten Have, 2007), 39.

6. A. Grün, *Kom naar de bron* (Amsterdam: TerraLannoo, 2002), 100.

7. R. Timmermans, *Hunkeren naar rust. Pelgrimeren door de regel van Benedictus* (Kampen: Ten Have, 2011), 190.

Additional resources and bibliography are available on
www.yourquietspot.com.

SCRIPTURE CREDITS

ABOUT THE AUTHOR

Former journalist Mirjam van der Vegt has been intrigued by silence and its use in the monastic traditions. During a difficult time in her life, she decided to dedicate herself to unraveling the mysteries surrounding silence. Over the years, she has written several books on the topic. She has led numerous retreats and training sessions in which participants learn to bring mindfulness, peace, and contemplation into their personal daily practice.

www.mirjamvandervegt.nl

www.training.mirjamvandervegt.nl

INSPIRATION FOR QUIETUDE

To accompany this book, you can download a beautiful poster that contains quotes to help you lay a foundation of quietude in your life. Mirjam van der Vegt takes you on a creative path in remembering the lessons of *Stilte*.